successful
Container
Gardening

CREATIVE
HOMEOWNER®

successful
Container
Gardening

75 Easy-to-Grow Flower and Vegetable "Gardens"

BY JOSEPH R. PROVEY

CREATIVE HOMEOWNER®, Upper Saddle River, New Jersey

PRODUCED BY HOME & GARDEN EDITORIAL SERVICES

PROJECT MANAGER	Joseph R. Provey
COPY EDITOR	Owen Lockwood
PHOTO RESEARCH	MaryAnn Provey
INDEXER	Home & Garden Editorial Services

CREATIVE HOMEOWNER

VICE PRESIDENT AND PUBLISHER	Timothy O. Bakke
MANAGING EDITOR	Fran J. Donegan
ART DIRECTOR	David Geer
SENIOR EDITOR	Kathie Robitz
PRODUCTION COORDINATOR	Sara M. Markowitz
JUNIOR EDITOR	Angela Hanson
SENIOR GRAPHIC DESIGNER	Glee Barre
PHOTO COORDINATOR	Mary Dolan
DIGITAL IMAGING SPECIALIST	Frank Dyer
COVER DESIGN	Glee Barre

Current Printing (last digit)
10 9 8 7 6 5 4 3 2 1

Manufactured in the United States of America

Successful Container Gardening, First Edition
Library of Congress Control Number: 2008942322
ISBN-10: 1-58011-456-3
ISBN-13: 978-1-58011-456-1

CREATIVE HOMEOWNER®
A Division of Federal Marketing Corp.
24 Park Way
Upper Saddle River, NJ 07458
www.creativehomeowner.com

Planet Friendly Publishing
✓ Made in the United States
✓ Printed on Recycled Paper
Text: 10%   Cover: 10%
Learn more: www.greenedition.org

GREEN EDITION

At Creative Homeowner we're committed to producing books in an earth-friendly manner and to helping our customers make greener choices.

Manufacturing books in the United States ensures compliance with strict environmental laws and eliminates the need for international freight shipping, a major contributor to global air pollution.

And printing on recycled paper helps minimize our consumption of trees, water, and fossil fuels. *Successful Container Gardening* was printed on paper made with 10% post-consumer waste. According to the Environmental Defense Fund Paper Calculator, by using this innovative paper instead of conventional papers we achieved the following environmental benefits:

Trees Saved: 23

Water Saved: 10,432 gallons

Solid Waste Eliminated: 633 pounds

Greenhouse Gas Emissions Eliminated: 2,166 pounds

For more information on our environmental practices, please visit us online at www.creativehomeowner.com/green

Dedication

To my friends at the Black Rock Garden Club in Bridgeport, CT, whose encouragement, suggestions, and contributions helped make this book possible.

Acknowledgments

This book would not have been possible without the help of Kate Parisi, whose container designs and ideas grace many of the following pages, and Master Gardener Ruth Zelig of The Pot de Deck in Bridgewater, NJ, who contributed container designs and photos, and read the manuscript for technical accuracy. Other generous contributors include: Joanna Guzzetta of Four Seasons Container Gardens in Portland, OR; Chicago Specialty Gardens of Evanston, IL, Campo de' Fiore of Sheffield, MA; Master Gardener Julie Sedwick; Marilyn Thorkilsen; and Bob La Pointe. Special thanks to Netherland Bulb Information Center/North America and Proven Winners for sharing many of their container recipes and photos.

Safety First

A‍ll projects and procedures in this book have been reviewed for safety; still it is not possible to overstate the importance of working carefully. What follows are reminders for plant care and project safety. Always use common sense.

- Always use caution, care, and good judgment when following the procedures described in this book.
- Always determine locations of underground utility lines before you dig, and then avoid them by a safe distance. Buried lines may be for natural gas, electricity, communications, or water. Start researching by contacting your local building officials. Also contact local utility companies; they will often send a representative free of charge to help you map their lines. In addition, there are private utility locator firms that may be listed in your yellow pages. Note: Previous owners may have installed underground drainage, sprinkler, and lighting lines without mapping them.
- Always read and heed tool manufacturer instructions, especially the warnings.
- Always ensure that the electrical setup is safe; be sure that no circuit is overloaded and that all power tools and electrical outlets are properly grounded and protected by a ground-fault circuit interrupter (GFCI). Do not use power tools in wet locations.
- Always wear eye protection when using chemicals, sawing wood, pruning trees and shrubs, using power tools, and striking metal onto metal or concrete.
- Always consider nontoxic and least-toxic methods of addressing unwanted plants, plant pests, and plant diseases before resorting to toxic methods. When selecting among toxic substances, consider short-lived toxins, those that break down quickly into harmless substances. Follow package applications and safety instructions carefully.
- Always read labels on chemicals, solvents, and other products; provide ventilation; heed warnings.
- Always wear protective clothing, including a face mask and gloves, when working with toxic materials.
- Never employ herbicides, pesticides, or other toxic chemicals unless you have determined with certainty that they were developed for the specific problem you hope to remedy.
- Never work with power tools when you are tired or under the influence of alcohol or drugs.
- Never carry sharp or pointed tools, such as knives or saws, in your pockets.

Contents

This Container "Garden" Includes

- 2 Bugleweed, *Ajuga reptans* 'Black Scallop'
- 3 Orange Sedge *Carex testacea*
- Strawflower *Chrysocephalum apiculatum* 'Flambe Yellow'
- Coral Bells *Heuchera* 'Dolce Creme Brulee'
- 20-in.-dia. urn

Introduction

Several years ago, upon moving into a house with a small yard, I was introduced to container gardening. Don't get me wrong: there is nothing I love more than working the ground and getting real soil on my hands, but with limited space—and the accumulation of years—container gardening has become a passion for me. I like that I can put my favorite plants where I spend time outdoors—on my deck, on my porch, and beside my favorite lounge chair. I enjoy the foliage and flowers every time I enter or leave the house—or take a meal outdoors. Being able to step outside for sage or basil to add to an omelet or pizza is a real joy, too. Having my plants nearby also allows me to tend to them more easily. I find I keep up with weeding and watering, and I spot problems in my containers sooner than I do in my in-ground garden.

I also like the fact that I can grow a wider variety of plants in containers than in the ground. Container plants are easier to adapt to a wide range of growing zones because they don't have to be hardy enough to survive cold winters. I can also tailor the potting mix to the plants' needs, regardless of the type of soil around my yard. These, of course, aren't the only advantages to container gardening. If you don't have a patch of ground for growing, container gardening lets you grow in small areas, such as balconies, patios, and courtyards. Renters can even take their gardens along when it's time to move. Container gardens are also great for children and the physically challenged. Set them on low benches, and they're at eye level and wheelchair accessible. They're good for elderly people who are not up to the rigors of an in-ground garden, too.

Container gardens are not foolproof. I've had my share of failures. More attention must be paid to watering and fertilizing plants in containers because they grow in a relatively limited amount of soil. But in many ways, plants in containers are more manageable than plants in the ground. You don't have to be able to wield a tiller or irrigate large areas. Animal pests, such as deer, are less likely to venture up the stairs to a porch or deck. And if you don't like the arrangement of your container garden, it's relatively easy to change.

In *Successful Container Gardening* you will learn everything you need to know to get started. It begins by showing various approaches to container gardening and gives tips on choosing containers and potting mix. The core of the book shows you how to plant from seed or flats and offers 75 "recipes" for containers that include plants you may never have heard of, as well as everyone's favorites. The final chapter is devoted to keeping your plants healthy. It delves into irrigation, fertilization, pruning, and handling diseases and pests.

Gardening is one of life's greatest pleasures. How often do you get the opportunity to surround yourself with beautiful living things? So give container gardening a try!

Using the "Recipes" in this Book

Plant Names

Hardiness and Heat Zones

Exposure

Full Sun to Partial Sun

Urn Your Salad

Spring is a time for celebration. Have some fun by mixing edibles with early ornamentals, as Kate Parisi did here.

- 4 lettuce *Lactuca sativa* mix of 'Salad Bowl' and 'Buttercrunch' (V) (NA, 12–1)
- 3 kale *Brassica oleracea* (V) (7–1, 6–1)
- 3 pansies *Viola* any pale blue cultivar (A) (9–1, NA)
- 3 grape hyacinth *Muscari aucheri* 'Blue Magic' (B) (6–0, 9–5)
- 3 golden creeping Jenny *Lysimachia nummularia* (P) (4–8, 8–1)
- Potting mix, light fertilization
- Pot or urn, 10-in. depth (min.)

How to Pot

Plant the grape hyacinth in the center of the pot or urn. Then surround it with kale and lettuce. Fill openings with pansies and creeping Jenny.

This "recipe" is on page 104.

Each of the 75 "recipes" contains all the information you'll need to duplicate the design. There is a photograph of the finished container, the correct exposure for the plants used, the number and types of plants in the container, and important growing information.

Containers allow you to change your plants' positions as needed, giving them more or less sun and shelter from the wind. They can also bring a dash of color into an early-spring garden, such as this combo of viola, hyacinth, and edibles.

Chapter 1

Choose Your Gardening Style

There are at least three ways to enjoy container gardening. The most popular, and easiest for beginners, is to decorate outdoor living areas with plants in pots, baskets, and planters. These miniature gardens add stunning colors, lush foliage, intriguing shapes, and sometimes fragrance to decks, porches, and patios. In addition, putting your green creations near the front door is a great way to welcome visitors.

he second way to garden in containers is to grow edibles. Virtually any vegetable, herb, fruit, or berry you can grow in the ground can also be grown in a pot or planter. While the goal of growing food is usually the harvest, not decoration, containers filled with edibles can be quite attractive. Many of the container "recipes" beginning on page 66 combine ornamentals with herbs and vegetables for attractive displays that would look good anywhere in the yard.

The third way to use planted containers is in landscaping. Here, the pots and planters go well beyond decoration and food production. The goal is to create gardens in the truest sense of the word—places that intrigue, inspire, and encourage rest and meditation. Such undertakings

typically require some design skills, or at least a "good eye." They are what landscape architects and designers study for years to do. But with some help, you can create beautiful backyard landscapes that make use of containers, too. The nice thing about designing with containers is that if your completed landscape is not to your liking, making changes is relatively easy. You'll only need to move some containers—not uproot plants.

Homeowners can enjoy all three approaches to container gardening at the same time: decorating a porch or entry; growing edibles on a deck or patio; and placing accents, focal points, and other elements in a landscape. But more often than not one style dominates. Which is right for you? Let's look at each one more closely.

Colorful railing planters (above) are a quick and easy way to put color where you can see it every day.

Colorful ornamentals in pots keep this large deck from looking empty and barren (right).

Decorating with Planters

Man-made outdoor spaces often look barren and unnatural. Add container plantings, and suddenly a deck or patio comes to life. Hanging baskets are, of course, a quick way to brighten up a porch. But also consider placing baskets (especially large, heavy ones) on the ground. I set mine on ring stands or tripods fashioned from cut branches.

Placing containers by the front door, usually in pairs, is perhaps the most popular way to decorate with planted containers. Scale is the key to success here. Don't purchase urns that will dominate the entrance. Of course if you live in a Georgian colonial with a grand entrance, small containers are going to look silly.

Another way to decorate an outdoor living area is with large bowl-shaped containers placed on outdoor tables. This past spring and summer I enjoyed the oxalis and nasturtium combination on my outdoor dining table. The container recipe is on page 70. A fringe benefit was being able to eat the leaves and flowers in summer salads.

Other great spots for containers are along deck and porch balustrades and at the base of stairways. The repetitiveness of these architectural elements almost demands the twist of a vine or a spray of flowers. Avoid the temptation, however, of putting pots on stair treads where they may prevent visitors from being able to grasp the handrail.

Planters are a natural choice for decorating outdoor kitchens and pool areas, too. Use them to soften the hard edges of outdoor cabinetry, grills, hot tubs, and the like.

A house dominated visually by two or three garage doors can be instantly enhanced by placing a large planter between the bays. (Just don't choose a woody-stemmed plant that could scratch your car.) Other ungainly features that you may want to screen from view include basement

Gardener's Tip

Avoid overdoing it. Remember that container gardening, despite its many advantages, requires you to pay closer attention to watering and fertilization than ground-based gardening.

hatchways; HVAC equipment; concrete stoops; retaining walls; utility sheds; electrical boxes, conduit, and meters; propane tanks; and oil fill pipes.

Container plantings can also be used to soften or hide undesirable views. Want to block the view of the kids' backyard soccer pitch or baseball diamond? Or of the neighbor's compost bin? Container plantings can help. Similarly, you may want to screen the view of a pool or spa from your more formal outdoor dining area.

Relieve the monotony of double or triple garage doors (above) with container boxes placed between the bays.

Gardener's Tip

Keep flowering baskets looking great by turning them often so the shaded side of sun-loving plants doesn't become leggy. Swivel hooks make it easy.

Use potted plants (left) to soften hard architectural lines and to alleviate unbroken, boring expanses of masonry or siding.

Potted plants at the entry door (opposite) are a great way to draw attention and welcome guests to your home. Concrete urns, such as these, are a good choice for formal entryways.

Growing Edibles

A patio or deck that's close to the kitchen is a great place to put containers filled with herbs, especially if you're like me and enjoy dashing outside for some sprigs as you're getting ready to make an omelet, pizza, or salad. Herbs are pretty, too. They mix readily with flowering plants and won't interfere with the decor.

Vegetables have a place in a patio garden, too. Many are quite decorative in their own right. Select compact varieties you can control, such as cherry tomatoes and lettuce, as well as pole beans, cucumbers, and squashes you can train on trellises or on strings. Mix them with annual flowers to add interest to the display. On pages 104-113 you'll find many container "recipes" that combine flowers and vegetables.

If you're interested in growing large veggies in containers, such as bush squash, melons, and full-size tomato plants, you may want to choose a location that's less visible from the patio or deck where you do your entertaining. Then again, you may prefer to lounge by the pool and watch your corn and tomatoes ripen. In either case, there are plenty of easy solutions. My preference is to keep vegetables near the house but to group the containers where they won't clash with my other arrangements. The back or side of a deck, or alongside a south-facing garage or shed wall, are good locations for large-vegetable containers.

Grouping your edible-plant containers together also makes for convenient watering and cultivation. Arrange them so that you can reach every plant and one group does not shade another. If space is tight and you're having trouble keeping every plant in the sun, build a wooden or masonry "terrace," or simply raise the back row of plants off the ground using an old bench or cinder blocks.

Making the Conversion

Want to try a very large vegetable garden in containers? There are many gardeners, including some commercial growers, who have converted their in-ground vegetable gardens to container gardens. Containers can be used to grow nearly any vegetable. Large 5-gallon buckets, wooden boxes, and self-watering plastic troughs are the containers of choice for such gardens.

Humor, beauty, and good pickings combine in this charming backdoor vignette (opposite). Pick the lettuce until it bolts in hot weather, and then replace it with purple pod beans and petunias.

Big Producers for Small Spaces

Carrots grow well in containers that are at least a foot deep. Two square feet will yield about 25 carrots.

Chard, an ideal container plant, is compact, has pretty foliage that even comes in colors, and regrows after a cutting.

Container Landscaping

Container gardening offers design possibilities that go well beyond ornamentation and food production. Designers use planted containers, along with in-ground plants and out-door structures, to create total garden environments, often described as "outdoor rooms." For example, planted containers used in combination with trellises, pergolas, and arbors can be used to grow "walls" and even leafy "ceilings." Such get-away-from-it-all arrangements afford shade and privacy and filter out street noise.

Planted containers can also serve as focal points, accents, borders, and barriers. The purpose of a focal point or accent is to draw the eye of the viewer and to say *This is important or special, and it's where I want you to look.* A single planted container in a garden bed or a grouping of containers can do the trick. Make your planted container more prominent by raising it on a pedestal, a pier of stones, or bricks. Planted birdbaths are another fun way to create a focal point, but don't forget to allow for drainage. (Use a masonry bit to bore the drainage holes—they can always be replugged later if you want a birdbath again.)

Container-planted borders and barriers can help with backyard traffic control, path definition, and safety. Borders show guests where to walk—and where not to walk. Use them to direct viewers to a path. Barriers, of course, prevent movement altogether. Use them to cordon off areas where you don't want traffic, such as near a steep drop in terrain, along the open edge of a deck, or behind a barbecue grill in a yard where young children play.

Container gardens can be an antidote for the architecturally challenged home, adding relief or dimension to an otherwise boring exterior. If there is something you just

Place your thumb over the urn in the top photo—it's located lower left on the opposite page. Remove it to see how important this vertical element is to the landscape.

Pots of tulips (right) are a spectacular way to beckon visitors to explore a spring garden.

Creating a garden is like writing a good story. Don't give away the ending in the first chapter.

don't like about the look of your house, camouflage it! I once owned a ranch-style home where the front was long, boring, and unrelieved by architectural features of interest. Several large cedar containers and a small bluestone patio in the front yard created the depth and variety it needed.

Transitions and Buffers

Another way designers use container plantings is to help with transitions. Carefully chosen, they can make decks, porches, and patios feel as if they are as much a part of the yard as they are of the house. Here, the goal is often to blur the transition from hard-scaped areas, such as decks, to the yard. Conversely, in urban settings, containers serve as buffers to hard-edged cityscapes of concrete and asphalt. In both cases, container gardens allow you to feel as if you're sitting in the middle of a garden, while having the comfort and convenience of a level floor underfoot.

An easy way to create a transition is to fill containers with plants that are already growing in your yard. The eye of the viewer will automatically connect the two spaces.

In urban settings (above and opposite) container gardens help create an oasis of green and can offer a sense of privacy.

Containers in a suburban yard (below) ease the change from house to yard. They also help define the outdoor "rooms."

Pairing Containers and Trellises

Trellis-grown plants are a useful element when creating outdoor living spaces, but sometimes it's not possible or desirable to plant in the ground where you'd like to have a trellis. In such cases, you may plant your vines or other climbers in containers. Be sure the containers are large and heavy. Vines dehydrate quickly on hot, sunny days, so they'll need plenty of potting mix to help keep roots moist. A weighty container will help prevent top-heavy vines from blowing over in strong winds. Vines are heavy feeders, too, so be sure to read about how to make supplemental feedings every two weeks throughout the growing season with a water soluble fertilizer.

Popular container-grown vine and climber suggestions include climbing hydrangea (above), clematis (top right), and passion flower (right). Wisteria, mandevilla, and climbing roses (not shown) also work well in many growing zones.

For example, if you have a large mass of perennials planted near your patio, put the same or similar species on your deck. For a no-cost way to do this, wait until it's time to divide your perennials, and then fill some containers to create an on-deck garden that echoes the surrounding beds.

Create buffers with dense, hedge-like shrubs or with trellises. In addition to the classic boxwood, potted hollies, yews, and arborvitae make beautiful buffering shrubs. For trellises, there are many wonderful choices, including mandevilla (Brazilian jasmine) with its glossy green foliage and large, colorful blossoms. My wife's favorites for the trellis on our deck are moonflowers. They have white, saucer-size blossoms that open at evening time.

Gardener's Tip

Can't afford a large urn? Stack several concrete blocks and set a large pot on top. Level and tamp the ground under the blocks to ensure stability. Hide the blocks with plants.

A Victorian urn (below) creates a vertical element that counterbalances the horizontal shape of the water feature in this yard.

Chapter 2

Selecting Pots and Planters

Most people select containers based on style and price. These qualities are important, but there are other factors to consider, including weight, size, shape, and scale. For example, you'll want to avoid large, heavy containers if moving them will be an issue. Lightweight containers, on the other hand, may not be suitable if you live in a windy location. And a massive concrete pot would probably overpower a planting of delicate, feathery ferns.

he size of the containers you choose will depend on the habit and number of plants you intend to grow—and, of course, how much space you have. Most plants come with information about their height at maturity and their space requirement. Keeping in mind that you can space plants closer in a container than you would in the ground, the container size should be about two-thirds the size of the mature plant or the combined size of a group of plants.

In general, the larger the container, the better it is for growing plants. Small containers hold less potting mix and therefore dry out more quickly, offer fewer nutrients, and heat up faster in the sun, often damaging the roots. Of course, large containers can be unwieldy

and, in some cases, too heavy for the deck or balcony.

The shape of a container should complement the habit, height, and shape of the plant. Imagine the overall contour of your plantings at maturity, and try to envision how they will look in the container. A densely planted mass of vinca will look good in a container that's about two-thirds the height of the plants, or about 8 inches tall. A shallow planter would suit Alpine flowers. An urn would complement the arching form of many ornamental grasses.

Container shape also impacts how frequently you'll need to water. If you buy a tall, slender container, the "water table" after irrigation may be quite low. While this may be fine for a drought-resistant succulent or a long-rooted plant like an ornamental grass, it could spell disaster

for shallow-rooted plants, such as many annuals and herbs, and foliage plants that like moist soil.

Scale, a function of plant and container size, is also important. The mass of the plants should be a bit more than the mass of the container for a balanced look. A large plant in a small container looks as awkward as a small plant in a large container. The scale of a container in its setting is also important. Large containers on a small deck will look odd.

Finally, container selection depends largely on your goals. If you're hoping to mimic nature and to create a ver-dant retreat on your patio, you'll probably be hiding the containers anyway. If this is the case, there's no reason to buy anything fancy or expensive. On the other hand, if you want to show off your containers or use them as design elements, whether for color or shape or theme, buy accordingly. I find pots less interesting than plants. My wife likes pots. So we compromise.

The container often makes the arrangement (right). Several of my favorite container gardens consist simply of one plant and just the right container. This fluted bowl is one of them.

Plants with a trailing habit (below) hide the container in which they're planted, creating a more natural, garden-like setting—and making the container less prominent.

Gardener's Tip

Mix one large container with smaller ones to add
instant height to a grouping of planters. Achieve a
similar effect by using bricks or stones to raise
one planter higher than its companions.

you have space in a shed or garage, move them inside. Simply leaving filled terra-cotta containers to the mercy of the elements will ensure their early demise.

Ceramic

Glazed ceramic containers, also called stoneware, come in many sizes. Large bowls are quite common. Ceramic containers are made from clays that are whiter and more finely textured than terra-cotta. They are also fired at hotter kiln temperatures, making them less porous and more resistant to damage from freezing. A bit more expensive than terra-cotta pots, glazed stoneware is available in every color of the rainbow. Many have cheerful designs brushed or molded onto their sides. Ceramic containers, because of their heft, are a good choice for top-heavy plants. They too, however, can crack if left exposed to freezing weather unemptied and unprotected.

A terra-cotta container (top left) allows moisture to migrate through its walls, keeping roots cool but requiring extra watering.

Mineral efflorescence and moss (opposite) only add to the charm of terra-cotta. The pot in front was pre-aged by the manufacturer, but you can add moss to any porous container. (See below.)

Coir to Concrete

Plant containers are made from a surprising variety of materials. Each has its advantages and disadvantages, with price being a big factor. The list below will give you a better idea of what will work best for your container garden.

Terra-cotta

A type of clay, this is a very common pot material. The warm red-brown color, classic shapes, affordability, and earthy appeal of terra-cotta make it a favorite with many gardeners. Pot sizes range from 2 or 3 inches to more than 2 feet in diameter. In addition to the vase shapes that have been popular for centuries, terra-cotta is used to make bowls, square pots, and rectangular troughs. Unlike other ceramics, terra-cotta is usually unglazed and therefore permeable. Douse a pot with water, and watch it get dark with the absorbed liquid. During hot weather, this will speed the loss of water from the potting mix—and the plants. For many plants, this is not necessarily a bad thing. After all, overwatering plants can be as bad as underwatering them. But if you find you can't keep up with your watering chores because your terra-cotta-potted (or concrete-potted) plants dry out too quickly, line the inside of the pots with sheeting from plastic trash bags (with holes for drainage), or brush the inside of the pot with a coat of gloss paint or varnish.

Because terra-cotta is more fragile than some of the other container materials, these containers should be emptied and stored upside-down if you live in a cold climate. If

Growing Moss

Bring your flowerpots to life—literally—with the beautiful green patina of moss. Growing moss on any porous container is not difficult, but it does require patience. Moss grows slowly, so it may take a few months to a year to get results.

To get started, pick some live moss and remove as much soil from it as possible. Next, blend it with yogurt, buttermilk, or beer and a teaspoon or two of sugar. Use a ratio of about one part moss to four parts liquid. It's easiest to do this in an electric blender, but you can also blend by hand. When the consistency is that of a very thick soup, spread it on your pots using a brush, a spatula, or your hands. Then place your pots in a cool, shaded area and mist the pot often to keep it slightly damp. The best containers for growing moss are unglazed clay, concrete, and hypertufa, a man-made material that looks like rock.

Wood

Wooden containers look at home in nearly any outdoor setting, especially on decks and porches. They are typically built in square or rectangular shapes, some small enough to serve as a window box and others large enough to hold a sizable tree. Halved wood barrels are also widely available.

Wood is a good insulator and is slow to dry out, so it's great for tempering extreme swings in the weather. It's also unlikely to crack during winter freezes. I have had great success keeping evergreens, including globe and picea spruce, for more than a decade in cedar boxes that measure 2 x 2 x 2 feet. Wood, even cedar, is susceptible to rot. Line the container's inside walls with sheet plastic or rubber, and avoid standing the containers directly on soil.

Wood enclosures, often called raised beds, are containers without the bottoms. Make them from 2x10 or 2x12 lumber, 3 to 4 feet wide and 6 to 8 feet long. On-ground enclosures combine all of the advantages of container gardening (better control of soil, mulching, weeding, and irrigation) with the advantages of in-ground gardening (greater area for roots, more access to water nutrients, and better drainage).

Plastics

Plastic containers come as troughs, baskets, and pots. The latter are available in the familiar utilitarian thin-wall plastics as well as in thicker polypropylene that can be made to look like terra-cotta or stoneware. Commercial growers favor plastic because of its low cost, durability, weight, moisture retention, and versatility. A dark-colored plastic, for example, will warm the soil during the day, enabling growers to extend the growing season of some plants both in the spring and fall. This may be helpful for northern gardeners who want to grow eggplants or tomatoes. It's less than ideal for gardeners in the Southwest who must worry about dark-colored plastics that can overheat plant roots.

Pressed Paper and Coir

Large pressed-paper containers are an economical choice for growing vegetables. Group them together behind your more ornamental containers, and you have the best of both worlds. Pressed-paper containers breathe like clay pots, which promotes healthy root development, improves aeration, and insulates roots from temperature fluctuations. These pots are biodegradable, which is good for the envi-

Be sure that any hypertufa or concrete planter you purchase or make is thoroughly cured before planting. New concrete will leach minerals, making soil too alkaline for many plants.

Material Choices for Containers

Polypropylene containers are impermeable and light-weight. These mimic glazed ceramic pots.

Wood is susceptible to rot, but the manufacturer claims that these teak containers will last 20 years.

Fiberglass containers resist gouges and scratching better than polypropylene, and look more realistic, too.

Metal frames are often lined with coco fiber to create hanging planters, such as the one shown here.

Metal urns are long-lasting and not damaged by freezes. Drainage is through the base.

Pots That Save Time

Self-watering containers are gaining in popularity, especially for edibles. They typically consist of a plastic container with a reservoir built into the bottom that is in contact with soil-filled channels. Fill the fill pipe with water, and within a day or so the potting mix will wick up the water and be thoroughly moist. Some self-watering containers include support systems for tall plants, outriggers for planter stability, and fabric mulch that snaps over the top like a shower cap. For more information on these containers, see page 134.

Self-watering containers are now available as window boxes, hanging baskets, pots, and troughs (shown). There are kits that fit existing pots, too.

This 12 x 12 x 30-in. model is suitable for large vegetables. It includes a fill tube, mulch screens, casters, potting mix, and a slow-release fertilizer.

ronment but means you will have to replace them yearly. Their low cost—less than $2—makes them very economical. Some pressed-paper containers are wax coated, which gives them a slightly longer life.

Another inexpensive and renewable option is a coir pot, which is made of coconut husks. These pots are sturdier than pressed-paper pots, with all of the same benefits.

EcoForms pots are made of grain husks with natural starch binding agents. They are inexpensive and come in a variety of colors and shapes up to 12 inches in diameter. EcoForm pots last five years under normal outdoor usage and are biodegradable.

Fiberglass

Fiberglass pots are made from a mix of glass fibers and resin. Typically, they are molded to look like terra-cotta or stone. In fact, some manufacturers actually add clay or limestone to the resin to create lifelike textures. Fiberglass pots are extremely durable and lightweight, and they do not have to be stored inside, even in cold climates. To my eye, they are more realistic looking than polypropylene containers—especially if the surface is textured.

Concrete

Concrete planters, once aged a bit, look at home in nearly any garden. They are available in very large sizes, making them perfect for large plants that need space to grow and ballast to stay where you put them. Wind will not budge them, nor are they apt to be pilfered from your yard! Conversely, don't plan on moving them often to rearrange your garden. Concrete is also a good insulator, moderating soil temperatures even on days with big swings in temperature. We've had a concrete urn in the family for more than 40 years, and it has survived winter after winter with only a single hairline crack.

Metal

A friend mentioned that there are two cast-iron planters in the front yard of a house that's been in his family for several generations. That's probably a testament to the material's two key characteristics: durability and weight. Aluminum containers are a more practical choice. They're nearly as durable, much lighter, and cost less. And they do not rust or need painting. Other metal options from which to choose include stainless steel (often copper coated), copper, lead, and zinc. All are expensive but long lasting.

Gardener's Tip

Plenty of containers and vessels that have outlived their original purpose can be converted to planters. Planters can be made from old wicker baskets, leaky galvanized buckets (above), watering cans, wheelbarrows—and even bathtubs and row-boats! Just keep your eyes open, and use your imagination.

Planter Types

There are nearly as many containers types as there are plants, each with their own special advantage. Check out the most common varieties below to find the ones that best suit your home and yard.

Boxes and Troughs

Made of wood, concrete, or various types of plastics, boxes and troughs use space more efficiently than do round containers. They also give roots more room to roam, with many holding more than 3 cubic feet of potting mix. Boxes and troughs are often the best way to make an architectural statement. Line them up, and you have a "wall." You can use them as barriers to keep people from walking where it may be dangerous, such as off the edge of a deck or on steps that have no railings.

Pots and Urns

Available in many sizes and made of various materials, pots and urns are ideal for grouping plants. You may use large and small pots together, and you can vary their heights by raising several above the others on blocks or pillars. Urns have a more formal look than pots and tend to be larger. They are often mounted on pedestals to create a focal point. Half urns, with one flat side, are a good way to conserve space on a small balcony or terrace.

Baskets

Baskets are usually made from plastic or metal frames and lined with pieces of sphagnum moss or coco-fiber matting. Some newer models are made from vinyl wicker. Baskets are the quickest way to make a splash with colorful annuals. You may also use them for herbs that have compact habits, such as sage, chives, thyme, and mint. Baskets do not take up much space and can be hung from just about anywhere, including tree

Troughs (top right) can be inserted in metal frames to serve as window boxes. Pots can be inserted in the same way.

Metal baskets (right), lined with sphagnum moss, make charming containers for a shady spot.

Gardener's Tip

Containers with saucers can contribute to root rot. The saucers collect water and cause the potting mix at the bottom of the container to become soggy. If you must use saucers, fill them with gravel before positioning your pot. That way, the pot will never sit in standing water.

Ensuring Drainage

Good drainage is important for most plants. Without it, the potting mix will stay saturated for long periods after rainfall or watering. Saturated soil has no space for air, which means your plants may suffocate. The remedy for this is simple. Make sure there are adequate drainage holes in your containers, and prevent them from clogging. In most types of containers, especially the large ones, I like to bore a couple of extra drain holes. Boring holes in fiberglass resin, wood, plastic, and most metals is easy using a standard twist-drill bit. A masonry bit will handle concrete and terra-cotta. For harder ceramics, you'll need a carbide-tipped bit. A drill with a hammer feature helps.

Before filling pots with potting mix, cover the drain holes with pot shards to help prevent plant roots from clogging them. Avoid using saucers or trays under pots. They're expensive and can contribute to overly saturated potting mix. If you feel that a saucer is necessary, fill it with gravel so the pot doesn't sit in water after a heavy rain. If you're worried about staining your patio or deck, raise pots using "pot feet" or small wood blocks. Even stones can work as pot feet. Raising pots makes it easier to sweep or hose debris from your deck or patio.

Pot shards shield drain holes from the roots that might otherwise clog them. Overly saturated potting mix can rot roots and harm your plants.

A wall-mounted garden panel can hold 22 quarts of potting mix in its 45 planting cells. Fully planted (above), the display can be striking. Mount on any wall or fence.

branches, eaves, porch ceilings, posts, and rafters. Be vigilant, however, baskets are exposed on all sides, top, and bottom, so they tend to dry out quickly. I discuss several techniques for lessening the risk to plants due to a forgetful gardener on pages 132–135.

Wall-Hung Planters

Wall-hung planters are a good way to add some life to an outdoor masonry wall or fence. Made from resins or fiberglass and resin, they tend to be small and must be watered frequently. They may also be hung from a post or trellis.

Garden panels are also available. (See the photo above.) Panels are molded from recycled plastic and include many soil "cells," or pockets, in which you can plant any number of different plants. Popular in Europe, they are used to create vertical gardens on balconies, terraces, courtyards, and other small spaces.

Window Boxes

Window boxes are usually hung from the framing of an exterior wall. They can be made from any of a number of materials, including woven vinyl wicker, fiberglass and resin, solid plastic, and fiber-lined metal frames. Most, however, are constructed from wood into which you insert plastic liners or individual pots.

Rail Planters

Similar to window boxes but designed to adorn deck and porch balustrades, rail planters are another good way to put plants nearby without using up deck or patio space. Rail planters can either hang from or rest on balustrade rails.

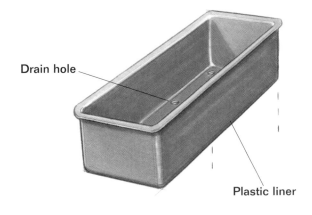

Drain hole

Plastic liner

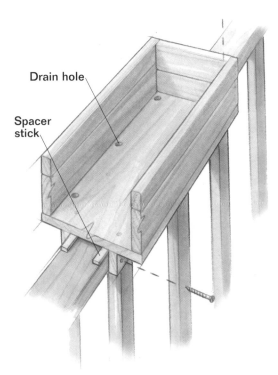

Drain hole

Spacer stick

If you build a rail planter, buy a plastic liner first and use it to determine your planter dimensions. This plan includes braces for stability. And don't forget to bore drain holes!

Container Styles

Container styles can be broadly grouped into three categories: traditional, minimal, and eclectic. Traditional pots and containers range from metal and concrete urns that reference classical designs to wooden troughs and boxes. Most come in natural or earthen colors and subdued patinas, although some glazed ceramic containers are decorated with colorful images. Traditional styles are often mimicked by containers molded from plastic resins.

Minimal-style containers lack ornamentation, but their simple shapes can make bold, architectural statements. Such containers are often made of metal, ceramics, and plastic resins, and come in many colors.

Eclectic containers can take any shape and are often whimsical—a ceramic pot made to look like a hollow log, a concrete fixture in the image of a Greek god, or a masonry container made to look like a wishing well. Found objects that have outlived their usefulness, such as an old bucket or boot, are also examples of eclectic containers. Too often, I fall in love with a pot and purchase it, and then am faced with finding a location for it. An easier way is to decide on the location and what you intend to plant, and then search for an appropriate pot. You may even want to bring a snapshot of the chosen spot when you go container shopping. The container location will give you clues as to what style container to purchase. For example, perhaps there is a nook on your deck between two wooden benches that will dictate shape, dimensions, and wood type. Or maybe your patio furniture has lots of curvy wrought iron and you'd prefer a curvy pot to match. If your home has a distinct historical style, you may want to limit yourself to planters that evoke the same period. Of course, your own personal preferences will enter the equation. While one gardener may prefer a simple geometric look to offset a chaotic jumble of blossoms, another may choose to use the containers to introduce additional shapes, colors, and textures to an outdoor space.

This traditional Asian-style container (foreground left) blends with surrounding plants, whereas minimally styled steel containers (opposite top) become as important as the plants they hold.

Gardener's Tip

Plastic pots, in direct sun, can overheat roots. Place the pot in a second container, called double potting (right), to shield it from sunlight. Double potting is also useful when you have a decorative pot with no drain holes, but remember to tip out the excess water frequently.

Making Your Own Hypertufa Container

Tufa is a soft rock that was once carved into troughs for water for livestock. Today, the old stone troughs are prized as planters. Hypertufa is a man-made material that substitutes for the real thing. It can be made to look aged by distressing the surfaces and allowing moss and lichen to grow on them.

To make your own hypertufa container, pick out a mold. Polystyrene, cardboard, or plastic work best because the hypertufa mixture will not stick to them. Begin with a modest-size mold of a couple of square feet before tackling a large project. If you use wooden or metal molds, line them with plastic; otherwise, the mixture will stick to your mold and damage your planter during removal.

There are several methods for making a hypertufa container. The one shown in the photos (opposite) nests one mold inside another. The gap between the nested molds should be 1 to 2 inches, or a bit larger for very large containers. MaryAnn, my wife, used plastic tubs as molds. Other possibilities include old basins, buckets, plastic pots, or polystyrene chests.

There are many recipes for making the hypertufa mix, but here is the one MaryAnn uses:

1 part Portland cement
1 part peat moss
1 part perlite or vermiculite
1 part sand

If you use vermiculite, it adds a bit of sparkle. Perlite adds flecks of white. Some recipes do not include sand and produce lighter containers. We use sand because it makes the hypertufa more durable. Adding a handful of fiber mesh will also increase strength. Purchase it at a masonry products supplier.

When mixing hypertufa ingredients, wear vinyl gloves, a dust mask, and safety goggles. Portland cement is caustic and should be rinsed from skin or eyes immediately.

Once you have finished molding your container, you can decorate the rim by pressing stones, shells, or leaves into the still-wet hypertufa. Then cover it with sheet plastic, and leave it in a shaded area. After 24 to 48 hours, remove the plastic and distress the container to your liking with any combination of cold chisel, wire brush, old paint scraper, and old kitchen fork. The hypertufa container will still be soft enough to shape at this point, but handle it with care because it can easily crack, too. Once you have the container looking the way you want, mist it with water, cover it with plastic, and allow it to cure for another day or two. Because hypertufa is alkaline while it's curing, hose it regularly for several weeks before planting.

Materials

■ Portland cement
■ Sphagnum peat moss
■ Plastic tub (approximately 16 x 19 in.)
■ 10-qt. plastic tub (with rim cut off)
■ Washed sand
■ Perlite or vermiculite

Distress container (right) with an old fork or wire brush. To round off edges or remove excess material, use a cold chisel.

1 Thoroughly mix sand, peat moss, perlite, and Portland cement in a large wheelbarrow.

2 Make a well; fill it with water; and mix ingredients. Continue adding water and mixing until you reach mud-pie consistency.

3 The mixture is ready when little or no water oozes out when you form a ball.

4 Add a 2-in. layer of the mixture to the bottom of the big plastic tub.

5 Make drain holes using wooden dowels.

6 Place the small tub in the center of the larger one. Fill around edges with mix, and allow to cure.

Chapter 3

Perfect Potting Mixes

Don't be like me. When I first began growing plants in containers, I resisted the idea of buying potting mix. After all, I had all the rich soil and compost I needed in my backyard. What I didn't know was that garden soil performs differently in containers than it does in the ground. Its structure becomes compact to the point where it no longer holds enough air for healthy plant growth. My clay-laden soil was an especially poor choice.

ontainer gardens are best grown in potting mixes that contain little or no soil. Potting mixes are engineered to drain well; to stay loose and not get compact; and to retain tiny air pockets, water, and nutrients. They are dense enough to anchor roots securely but lightweight for easy handling of large containers. And unlike soil from the garden, potting mix is sterile, minimizing the danger of plant disease and insect infestation.

Commercial, premixed potting mixes are made from a wide variety of materials, depending on the manufacturer and region. Traditionally, peat moss has been the key ingredient. It holds both water and air well and does not decompose quickly. It also has a high cation exchange capacity (CEC), which means that it holds nutrients well.

Particles with low CEC, such as sand, allow nutrients to leach out of the mix quickly. The high acidity of peat moss (pH 3.5 to 4.0) is often adjusted with limestone.

There are several types of peat. The top performer is sphagnum peat moss, which would be more appropriately called sphagnum moss peat because it's formed from the decomposed sphagnum moss that builds up slowly in bogs. Fresh sphagnum moss is the same plant that is often used to line hanging baskets.

The name notwithstanding, sphagnum peat moss ranges in color from light brown to black. The darker the sphagnum peat moss, the more advanced its decomposition. Younger, lighter-colored peat moss does a better job of providing air space than do older, darker peats. Peat

also forms from the decomposed remains of other plants, including reeds, sedges, and grasses. These peats are not considered as desirable as sphagnum peat moss and may be difficult to rewet once dry. In addition, they are often harvested from environmentally sensitive areas.

As peat moss becomes more difficult to obtain, it becomes more expensive. As a result, researchers are seeking other ways to formulate potting mixes. Experiments have been done with bark, composts of various kinds, and biosolids, with varying degrees of success.

Potting Mix Ingredients

Here is a list of some of the other ingredients you may find in the potting mixes available at your home and garden center or from your local nursery.

Soil: The trend in potting mixes has been moving away from using soil as an ingredient. It may carry diseases or be

Sphagnum peat moss absorbs 10 to 20 times its weight in water and is a key ingredient to many potting mixes.

contaminated with pesticides. Sources for soil vary, and so does its quality. This makes it difficult to ensure product consistency. You may, however, find commercial potting mixes and mix-your-own recipes that include soil. Check with the supplier to be sure it is from a clean source that does not contain pesticides and that it has been sterilized.

Ground bark: Various tree barks, depending on what's locally available to the manufacturer, are often ground and substituted, in part, for peat moss in today's potting mixes. Bark lightens the mix when compared with peat but lowers its water retention. Pine bark performs best. Particles ground from pine bark create air spaces for healthy roots, retain moisture, and help to hold whatever nutrients have been added to the mix. Avoid hardwood bark unless it has been composted.

Calcined clay: Quarry clay, when heated, can be formed into a highly porous material. When crushed into small particles, it makes an excellent potting-mix ingredient. The particles are durable, provide pore space for air, retain water, and help to retain nutrients. It is especially suitable for potting mixes that will remain planted for long periods of time. Potting mixes with calcined clay tend to be more expensive than others.

Fibers: Potting mix can include any number of fibers, including Kenaf (a fibrous plant used to make paper), rice and peanut hulls, alfalfa, newspaper, and coir (a by-product of the coconut fiber industry). Such fibers are acceptable and may even have advantages over traditional ingredients. Coir, for example, holds more water and lasts longer than peat moss but is more expensive. It also contains more potassium, allowing you to reduce this element when fertilizing. On the other hand, it may contribute more salts to your mix because salt water is sometimes used in processing it. Sawdust, another fiber sometimes used in potting mix, is better if sourced from evergreens because softwood particles break down more slowly than hardwood particles. Avoid sawdust from cedar, walnut, and redwood because it can be toxic to plants. Avoid sawdust from oak, hickory, and maple because it ties up nitrogen.

Limestone: Growing media makers often include lime to raise pH levels to the desired range. Calcium carbonate and calcium magnesium carbonate, or dolomitic limestone, are the preferred forms and should be finely ground.

Perlite: Perlite is a naturally occurring volcanic rock. When crushed into particles and heated above 1,600 degrees F., the particles pop like popcorn and expand from 4 to 20 times their original volume. The expanded particles can hold three to four times their weight in water. Perlite is also lightweight, sterile, chemically inert, and pH neutral. It helps to retain nutrients and keep potting soil aerated.

Polystyrene foam: Beads and flakes of polystyrene are generally used as a cost-saving alternative to perlite in potting mixes. Polystyrene does not retain moisture or nutrients but does improve drainage. It is lightweight and durable but can be annoying to handle because the particles have a tendency to either drift in the wind or stick to hands and tools because of their static charge.

Protecting Peat Bogs

Peat moss bogs grow less than half an inch in a decade and take thousands of years to form. They also store carbon that would otherwise be released into the atmosphere and are therefore helpful in the effort to stem global warming. To ensure that this valuable resource is not over-harvested, buy only from certified suppliers. When possible, I prefer to use Canadian sphagnum peat moss. The Canadian Sphagnum Peat Moss Association (CSPMA) has adopted a Preservation and Reclamation Policy that sets out procedures for opening, harvesting, and closing bogs responsibly. Look for the CSPMA logo when buying peat moss. Other types of peat, such as sedge peat, may not be responsibly harvested.

The uppermost layer of sphagnum peat moss is first harrowed and then, once dry, collected with a large vacuum harvester.

Without intervention, which includes replanting and water management, peat bogs are unlikely to reestablish themselves once peat extraction is complete. A restored bog is shown above.

Using Less Mix

Filling a large container with potting mix can be costly. It's also unnecessary for many plants because the roots won't go much deeper than 12 inches. Instead, fill the bottom of a container with nonabsorbent materials, such as pieces of polystyrene packing, empty plastic bottles (caps on), or filler products made for container gardening. (See below.)

Packing Pearls are about the size of tennis balls. Use them to reduce container weight and improve drainage. (See Resources for more information.)

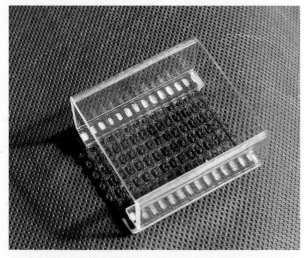

To prevent filler balls from obstructing drain holes, use the supplied drain shield. A permeable pot liner keeps mix and filler separate.

Vermiculite: Similar to but not as common as perlite, vermiculite is a mica-like mineral that expands when heated to a high temperature. In potting mixes, vermiculite improves soil aeration and moisture retention, is sterile, has a high CEC, and is close to pH neutral. If compressed while wet, however, vermiculite particles collapse and lose their shape. In addition, some mines that produced vermiculite in the past were found to contain asbestos. They are no longer in service, and clean, asbestos-free vermiculite is available at many home and garden centers.

Sand: Up to 10 percent of clean, coarse sand is sometimes added to potting mixes. It promotes good drainage. It also adds weight to the mix, which may be desirable for top-heavy plants, such as trees. Do not use beach sand because it's likely to have a high salt content. Clean, washed sand is available at most home centers.

Compost: Compost is a desirable supplement to potting mixes. It helps to retain moisture and sometimes provides nutrients as well. Composts found in potting mixes can be made from a variety of ingredients, including bark, fish waste, alfalfa, grass, and animal manures and bedding. Compost can also be made at home and used to make your own potting mix. (See "Making Your Own Compost," on page 54.)

Biosolids: Composted biosolids have also been successfully used in growing media in recent years. The city of Tacoma, WA, for example, offers Tagro Potting Soil, a mix of the city's treated biosolids, maple sawdust, and ground, aged fir bark. In tests conducted at the Washington State University Puyallup Research and Extension Center, Tagro products outperformed a commercial peat and manure mix. Its Tagro Potting Soil is even recommended for growing edibles, as its heavy-metal concentrations are well below the EPA-allowed limits. Avoid potting mixes that contain animal manures unless they have been well composted or rotted. They may rob plants of nitrogen and contain undesirables, including soluble salts, ammonia, weed seeds, insects, and pathogens.

Lighten your mix (opposite) with perlite, left, or vermiculite, right. Many potting mixes include one or the other for the purposes of improving aeration and retaining moisture.

Azaleas (above), hibiscus, boxwood, and blueberries benefit from an acidic potting mix. You can purchase an acidic mix or add elemental sulfur to your mix to lower the pH.

These tropical plants (left) prefer a potting mix with a high ratio of peat moss for moisture retention.

Fertilizer: There's not much nutritional value in many of the aforementioned ingredients, so some manufacturers have begun to add small amounts of fertilizers to their mixes. It's usually enough to see you through the first few weeks after planting. Percentages and the type of fertilizer vary. For additional information, see "Container Fertilization," on page 136, and "Fertilizer Basics," on page 138.

Types of Potting Mixes

There are lots of types of commercial potting mixes from which to choose. They vary depending upon the plants for which they are intended, the gardener's needs, and where the mix is manufactured. Mixes for annuals, for example, are engineered to hold moisture longer than mixes for succulents. Mixes for acid-loving plants, such as azaleas, blueberries, and evergreens, have a slightly lower (more acidic) pH. Mixes for cacti have a bigger dose of sand to ensure fast drainage and a higher (more alkaline) pH. Tropical plants and ones grown for foliage, on the other hand, prefer moist growing conditions. Specialized mixes for tropical plants will have more peat moss and fewer coarse particles.

Sometimes mixes are tailored to the needs of the gardener. Moisture-control mixes, for example, retain more water. They're helpful for gardeners who must be away from home regularly or those who live in hot, dry climates. Mixes that have fertilizer already added simplify container gardening for those who are pressed for time.

Potting mixes also vary by region because manufacturers typically use materials that are locally available. This practice reduces unnecessary shipping but means that a bag of potting mix in Maine is likely to have different contents from one from Louisiana—even if it's marketed under the same brand. Manufacturers claim that in terms of performance, however, the two bags will be very similar.

Buying Potting Mix

According to research done at Colorado State University (CSU), quality between potting mixes differs significantly. Based on results of container-planted geraniums and impatiens in garden centers around Colorado, products that include sedge peat performed poorly. Sedge peat is a fine-particle, low-porosity medium that does not drain water or hold air well. The researchers at CSU suggest looking for products that contain sphagnum peat moss instead. They also advise consumers to be sure they're buying a true potting media. Products that look similar to potting mix, such as compost, will yield poor results. Finally, the researchers say it's worth paying a little extra for quality mixes.

One way to get a quality potting mix is to go to a reputable nursery in your area and ask what it uses. Some nurseries will offer their suggestion for a good commercial blend. Others blend their own and offer it for sale, in which case they can tell you exactly what was used to make it. Another approach is to buy several small bags, each from a different manufacturer, and to compare the contents before buying more. You're likely to find significant differences. I was recently surprised to find one national brand loaded with twigs and big chips of wood. My son, who lives in a different part of the country, reported that his potting mix came with a collection of live insects—including gnats that proved tough to banish.

Gardener's Tip

For plants that require good drainage—succulents, cacti, and some herbs, for example—choose a potting mix with a high percentage of coarse particles, such as bark and perlite. For moisture-loving plants, such as many annuals, look for a mix with a high percentage of sphagnum peat moss.

Modifying a Potting Mix

When potting top-heavy plants, you may add clean, coarse sand to your potting mix. This will add weight for container stability but will not affect the mix's performance if you don't exceed 10 percent of the container volume. Conversely, if you're putting a large container garden on a roof deck, you may need to lighten your mix by adding perlite. Adding more than 20 percent of perlite, however, may cause your mix to drain too quickly.

The Importance of pH

The pH of potting media should be between 5.5 and 6.5 for most plants. If it's not, many plants will not be able to make full use of nutrients in the potting mix. Manufacturers of potting mediums take great pains to meet a desirable pH range, usually mixing in ground dolomitic limestone to counter the natural acidity of sphagnum peat moss. If you

plan to mix large amounts of your own potting mix, you may want to have it tested by your nearest Cooperative Extension Service. Simple pH testing kits are available at many garden centers, but they are less accurate.

When possible, test mixes before planting in them. It's much easier to adjust pH when you can thoroughly mix in the amendment as opposed to applying it to the surface. Use finely ground dolomitic limestone to make mixes more alkaline and elemetal sulfur to make them more acidic. Dolomitic limestone also contains the secondary nutrients calcium and magnesium. Add at rates suggested by the manufacturer, but keep in mind that it may take some time for the additives to have an effect, depending upon moisture levels, temperature, and size of the granules.

Hens and chicks (opposite) grow well in a potting mix with a neutral to slightly alkaline pH.

Checking pH at Home

Empty the capsule into the potting-mix sample; add water; shake; and allow the solution to settle.

Match the solution color to the supplied chart. This mix has a slightly alkaline reading of about 6.5.

Mixing Your Own

Potting mixes are expensive. Premium brands cost about $3 to $4 per cubic foot. You can mix your own and save money, but it's only worth it if you need more than 15 cubic feet and you don't mind the extra legwork required for locating the bulk supplies. You should also be inclined to experimentation. Several things have to be right for a potting mix to perform well, and you may not get the results you want on your first try.

If you use the wrong type of compost, for example, your plants may be robbed of nitrogen. If your mix is deficient in micronutrients, your plants may falter. Too much of some micronutrients, on the other hand, can cause problems, too. And to further complicate the issue, one major maker of potting mix admitted to me that it doesn't add micronutrients to its mixes because the trace elements are sufficiently available in the other ingredients.

I don't want to make this sound too complicated, because it's not. Plenty of on-line recipes are available to get you started. I've had good success with one published by the University of Florida. It calls for

6 gallons of sphagnum peat moss
¼ cup lime
4½ gallons vermiculite or perlite
4½ gallons compost

Mix thoroughly in a wheelbarrow, and add fertilizer according to the manufacturer's directions. If you want to make organic fertilizer, mix

2 cups colloidal rock phosphate
2 cups greensand
½ cup bone meal
¼ cup kelp meal

The best site I've found for plant-specific potting-mix recipes is plantideas.com.

Combine potting-mix ingredients in a large wheelbarrow (top right), and mix thoroughly with a shovel or hoe.

Add 1½ cups of fertilizer per batch of potting mix (right). Save the rest for feedings during the growing season.

A successful growing-medium mix must be able to retain water, air, and nutrients—and have a suitable pH.

Making Your Own Compost

Compost is a key ingredient in many potting-mix recipes that you create yourself. To make it, either buy or build a compost bin, such as the one shown on these pages, and begin to collect the ingredients listed in "What to Use."

Billions of microbes (fungi, bacteria, and tiny organisms) will help you turn these materials into compost, but you'll have to keep them happy with the right balance of moisture, air, and food. If you do, you'll be a successful compost maker. The moisture content of a compost pile or bin should be about 50 percent, or about as moist as a sponge that has been wrung (not dry or soggy). At less than 30 percent or more than

60 percent water, the process slows down. Air is necessary for the survival of aerobic microbes (those that need oxygen). Turn the contents and break the clumps in your pile with a garden fork to keep it well aerated. If you don't, you'll create conditions for anaerobic microbes. While they will also eventually break down organic materials, they produce odors.

Yard and kitchen waste is food to microbes. Add equal amounts of "green" waste (weeds, clippings, green leaves, fruit, manures, and vegetable scraps) and "brown" waste (dry and dead weeds, straw, wood chips, brown leaves, newspaper, and sawdust). Toss

on a soil "cap" between layers to guard against odors. Don't compost human or pet feces, meat, bones, diseased plants, walnut tree leaves or twigs, coal or charcoal ash, dairy products, fats or oils, or wood that has been treated with preservatives.

The compost bin below is easy to build. You'll need a saw, drill-driver, level, and a supply of galvanized screws. If you want a hinged lid for your composter, you'll also need strap hinges. Build one bin or several. Three is ideal because you can use one for fresh kitchen and yard waste, one for decaying material, and one for material that's nearly ready for use.

What to Use

- Animal manure
- Cardboard rolls
- Clean paper
- Coffee filters
- Coffee grounds
- Cotton rags
- Dryer and vacuum cleaner lint
- Eggshells
- Fireplace ashes
- Fruits and vegetables
- Grass clippings
- Hair and fur
- Hay and straw
- Houseplants
- Leaves
- Nutshells
- Sawdust
- Shredded newspaper
- Tea bags
- Wood chips
- Wool rags
- Yard trimmings

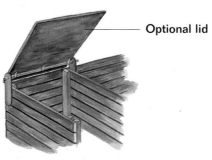

1x4 stabilizer

Space front stakes 1¼ in. apart so front boards will slide easily.

Removable 1x6 slats allow access to compost

2x2 pressure-treated stakes driven 1 ft. deep into the ground

Optional lid

This easy-to-build composter measures 3 x 4 x 9 ft. It is built with 2x2s and 1x6 boards. If you want a lid (left), use 2x4 rear posts and 1-in. conduit for the hinge. Attach the lid using electrical conduit clamps.

1 **Fasten stakes to 1x6 sideboards using galvanized wood screws, two per joint. Space the boards about ¾ in. apart.**

2 **Cut any excess length from tops of the stakes.**

3 **Drive stakes into level ground, protecting the stake tops with scrap wood to prevent splintering.**

4 **Check that stakes are vertical and that top boards are level.**

5 **Fasten the topmost back board to back stakes with galvanized wood screws. Check for level, and install the remaining back boards.**

6 **Slide front boards between the stakes. Add or remove boards as needed to contain or remove the compost.**

Chapter 4

Flowers, Vines, and Grasses

It's inspirational to walk through my local nursery in the spring, deciding which favorites I want back in my garden and which new varieties I'd like to get to know. But it can be overwhelming, too. There are unlimited flowers, vines, and grasses that can be grown singly or in combination in containers. Buy only after thinking about how you'll use the plants. Limit your day's purchases to what you can pot in an afternoon—or a weekend at most.

hen purchasing annuals, look past the blossoms and check the foliage for good color. If leaves are yellow or spotted, leave the flat behind. Ditto if plant development is uneven or if plants are leggy. Turn the tray or pot over and check whether roots have emerged from the drain holes. If they have in any great numbers, the plant may be root bound and you'll want to leave it behind. Or try popping it out of its container. If the plant has a solid fibrous mass of white roots, avoid it. Conversely, if the plant emerges from its container with a lot of soil spilling out, the roots may be underdeveloped.

Selecting healthy ornamental grasses and perennials is a little different. You're looking for good roots because they are what generate new growth every year. New, vigorous-looking shoots, with good color, are an indication of root health. Pot size is often a clue to root size. The bigger the better—and the more costly, too.

When planning your container garden, don't forget to check out the summer bulbs (including corms, tubers, and rhizomes, or roots). Some of the most stunning container plants begin with ungainly potato- or onion-like blobs, including calla and canna lilies, caladium, tuberous begonias, oxalis, and crocosmia. Bulbs are often sold loose, so you get to see what you're buying. Look for firm, well-formed specimens that feel heavy for their size. Avoid those with dark or light discoloration. Size is another indication of vigor. The bigger the bulb, the more food it has stored and the more likely it will produce blooms.

Getting Off to a Fast Start

Most of us enjoy seeing mature plants in at least a few out-door containers soon after spring arrives. One way to do this is to move plants you've overwintered indoors onto the patio as soon as the nighttime temperatures permit. It's wise to do this gradually to prevent plants from becoming burned by too much UV light or shocked by low temperatures. Putting plants in an unheated porch for a week or two, for example, is a good way to make the transition. Shading them from midday sun also helps.

Another approach to having colorful containers early is to plant spring bulbs in pots during the fall, allow them to overwinter in an unheated shed or garage, and to bring them out in the spring. (See the "recipe" on page 68.) Or dig up or purchase hardy mature plants, and slip them into a container. I like doing this with spring bulbs, such as daffodils and tulips, and with perennials, such as hosta and ferns.

Even before the lilies and hosta bloomed, this container was attractive and fun to watch—on May 10 (above, right), June 1 (right), and July 4 (opposite). The hosta bloomed in late July.

Layered bulbs (below) lengthen the display of an early-spring container. Plant the bulbs in the fall, and store them in an unheated place. After they have flowered, replant them in the garden.

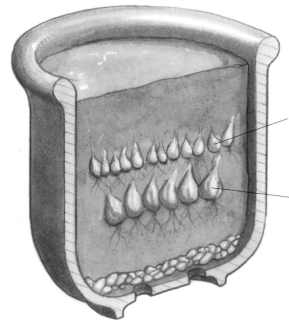

Early-blooming bulbs, such as narcissus

Later-blooming bulbs, such as tulips

Gardener's Tip

Forgot to plant your favorite bulbs last fall? To introduce spring colors quickly and easily, look in the supermarket for plants with healthy shoots and fully formed buds. Slip them out of their plastic pot and into a porch or deck container, adding more potting mix as necessary. Try not to disturb the roots, and water thoroughly.

Container Composition

There are lots of things to keep in mind when composing with plants in containers. If you already own the container, it will be your starting point. Whatever you put in it will have to work with the container's size, shape, and color. Small plants, for example, look better in small containers; big ones look better in bigger containers. Plants prized for their foliage often look better in a container with some color, and brightly colored flowers tend to show best in neutral-colored containers. Container shape can be a factor, too. I like to put plants with mounding habits in curvy planters and upright plants in square or rectangular containers, but there are no hard and fast rules. If you're buying a new container, you'll have fewer restrictions and will be able to choose a pot with a plant in mind.

The next consideration is that all the plants selected for a container must have similar sun, soil, and moisture requirements. Pairing a sun-loving plant with one that prefers shade is likely to cause problems. Some plants, like coleus, are quite adaptable to varying degrees of sun. Others aren't so easygoing.

Knowing the forms, or habits, of the plants you'd like to grow together is important, too, unless you're OK with the jungle look. Plant forms can be spiky, arching, climbing, mounding (clump), uniform, or cascading (trailing)—and a lot in between. Many irises and cordylines, for example, are spiky; grasses are often arching. Vines can climb or trail. Many woody-stemmed plants are upright or mounding, while some annuals are more uniform. (See the illustrations below.) Ask yourself whether the forms of the plants you select will complement each other and stay orderly or look awkward together and compete for space as they grow.

There are other characteristics to consider: color and size of foliage and blossoms, for starters. Then there's leaf shape, texture, and variegation. When I look closely at plants, I'm astounded by their diversity.

Plant forms, or habits, such as those shown in these illustrations, are the shapes that garden designers use to create interesting containers. When combining shapes, think about balance. Horizontal shapes can be balanced with verticals, trailing with upright, arching with spiky, and so forth.

Uniform

Arching

Spiky

Trailing

Mounding

Planting in Large Containers

1 Partially fill the urn and place the largest plant in the center so the root-ball top is about 1 in. below the rim.

2 Arrange other plants, while still in pots, around the center. Tops of all root balls should be at the same level. Rearrange until you're satisfied.

3 Working from the center of your arrangement, remove plants from containers and begin planting.

4 It helps to focus on one section at a time.

5 Fill between plants with potting mix. An empty plant pot can serve as a scoop, or use a trowel.

6 Water with a gentle stream. To see what this container looked like a few weeks later, go to page 73.

How Many Different Plants to Use?

One-plant containers, in which all the plants are the same species, are the easiest to design and often have the most impact. Even a planter filled with a grass or fern will give the eye a place to rest when placed in a garden bed or on a patio. To add a bit of variety to a monoculture, try including moss, shells, or an interesting stone to your container. Another way to create some variety in a one-plant container is to buy different cultivars from the same species. The difference may only be blossom color or plant size, but it's enough to create some diversity and interest.

You may also group several one-plant containers together to achieve the combination you like. There are several advantages to this approach: you can cater to each plant's needs individually; if one plant dies, you can replace it easily; and you can work with smaller, less-expensive containers.

Two-plant containers (containing at least one plant from each of two different species or genera) can be tricky. First, the plants must share similar needs with regard to sun, potting mix, and water. Second, two-plant containers tend to appear off-balance and awkward unless your choices complement one another perfectly.

What's in a Name?

Plants are classified in many ways, including family, order, class, and even tribe! Typically, two levels of classification are given in this book: the genus and the species. A genus is a plant group linked by a range of common characteristics. For example, *Papaver* is the genus name for poppies. Genus names are italicized, and the first letter is capitalized. A species is a member of a genus. Each species has some distinguishing characteristic, such as a different color blossom or leaf shape. Species names are italicized and printed in lower case. Together, the genus and species are usually enough to allow you to find that plant, or one similar to it, at your local garden center or by mail order. In cases where it is useful to have additional identification, cultivar or variety names are also given. Cultivars are cultivated varieties, usually derived from mutations or by hybridization. They differ from varieties (var.), which occur naturally in the wild. Cultivar names are set off by single quotes. Finally, common plant names are also provided as they are how most of us refer to plants.

Here is an example: when coreopsis is specified for the container "recipe" on page 70, it is listed as tickseed (the common name), *Coreopsis* (the genus), *auriculata* (the species) and 'Nana' (the cultivar). Note that in many cases, such as petunia, the common name and genus are the same.

A fairly safe approach is to use two species from the same genus. Here the differences are likely to be more pronounced than using differing cultivars, but they won't be widely dissimilar, either. Just remember that in any container composition, you're looking for ways to create a blend of the contrasts and commonalities.

Three-or-more-plant containers (at least one plant from each of three or more different species or genera) open up many possibilities. As with two-plant containers,

A neatly layered arrangement (left) requires careful attention to plant height and habit. This one begins with euphorbia 'Diamond Frost' and pink oxalis at the front, purple osteospermum in the middle, and umbrella plant topping off the group at the back.

A single-plant container (opposite) can be striking, as this planter box filled with trailing petunias illustrates.

Gardener's Tip

Perennials typically flower only once in the summer, some for longer periods than others. It's best, therefore, to mix them with annuals that bloom continuously during the season.

they must share similar sun, potting-mix, and watering needs. In addition, arranging many plants in the container demands more in the way of design skills. The conventional advice of container designers is to combine "thrillers," or attention-getters, with "fillers" and "spillers,"

plants that play supporting roles. Thrillers stand out and often have an element of surprise because of a showy blossom, vivid color, or unusual habit. Some examples of thrillers include canna, coleus, cosmos, dahlia, salvia, poppy, and zinnia. Fillers give an arrangement its shape

Loosening Root-Bound Plants

It is common to find that the plant you just purchased is root bound. Check before you buy, but if you're stuck with a root-bound plant, follow these steps.

Tear away large masses of roots at the base, and pull roots apart at the sides of the root ball. Be merciless. This will stimulate new root growth.

For a severely root-bound plant, cut away the bottom inch of root mass with the edge of a trowel or a knife. Then make several vertical cuts, and pull roots apart.

When buying plants, if possible, choose those with root density that looks like this. The roots are well developed but have not become a dense mat.

and body—calibrachoa, portulaca, and dusty miller, for example. Spillers, or trailing plants, cascade over a container's rim, softening its hard edges and helping the arrangement blend with other containers and the surrounding gardens. Cascading petunias, alyssum, thunbergia, verbena, and sweet potato vine are good spillers.

The thriller-filler-spiller formula is only one way to think about creating container designs. It often leads to predictable compositions, but it is helpful when you first begin creating your own container designs.

Another useful concept is the "centerpiece." It gives an arrangement its backbone, or structure. Borrowed from the art of floral design, centerpieces are usually upright or spiky and tall. They may also serve the thriller role in a container or act more as a backdrop for other plants. Tall ornamental grasses are often used as container centerpieces.

Three-or-more-plant containers often comprise more than a dozen plants. Consequently, they require large containers. (See "Planting in Large Containers" on page 61.) Containers with so many plants may be more difficult to control. Pinching and pruning may be necessary to prevent chaos!

When designing a multiple-plant container, it's helpful to begin with a theme. It can be a color you like, such as a pale frosty green foliage or flowers with sunset hues. It can be based on similar leaf shapes in varying sizes. Or you may choose to re-create something you've seen in nature, such as a vignette of woodland ferns and foliage, woodland flowers, or a group of desert succulents.

Symmetry and Balance

Arrangements with centerpieces are typically symmetrical. So are those planted with one or two varieties. Arrangements with several varieties can be symmetrical or asymmetrical. For a symmetrical arrangement, you have two choices: rings or rows. For the former, place the centerpiece in the center of your container; surround it with shorter mounding plants; and then plant low-growing trailing plants near the perimeter. If your container will only be seen from one direction, you may choose the "rows" approach. Plant the centerpiece to the center rear of the composition. Plant rows of fillers in front of it, tallest to shortest. Then plant spillers in front. In a large container you can opt for a less predictable arrangement. Place your tallest plant off center; then add mounding plants and trailing plants in ways that balance the arrangement.

Grouping one-plant and two-plant containers creates the effect of a much larger container planting—and is a lot easier, too. Here two pots of Autumn Joy Sedum buffer a lobelia and balloon flower pairing from a petunia and sweet potato vine combo.

Gardener's Tip

Grouping single-plant containers together allows you to combine plants that don't share the same preferences for moisture, pH, and nutrient levels. It also facilitates watering, shelters plants from the wind, and helps to reduce evaporation.

Ornamental Container "Recipes"

The "recipes" on the following pages provide container ideas and instructions for many types of annuals and perennials, including succulents, bulbs, and ornamental grasses. As with food recipes, feel free to make substitutions.

On the "marker" to the left of each "recipe" you will find the plants' preferred sun exposure. Exposures are defined as follows

> *Full Sun:* at least six hours of direct sunlight per day, with indirect (dappled or filtered) light for the remainder.
>
> *Partial Sun:* at least four hours of direct sunlight per day, with indirect light for the remainder.
>
> *Shade:* only two hours of direct sunlight per day, with indirect light for the remainder.

The "recipes" include plant names, potting mix and fertilization recommendations, pot sizes, and planting instructions. After each plant name, you'll find whether the plants are perennial (P); annual (A); bulb, corm, or tuber (B); cactus or succulent (C); herb (H); shrub (S); tree (T); or vine (V). Note: many tender perennials (plants that won't survive cold climates but would otherwise live for several seasons) are used as annuals. You'll also find

United States Department of Agriculture (USDA) hardiness zone ranges and American Horticultural Society (AHS) heat zone ranges. USDA hardiness zone ranges are listed in blue. They will help you determine how early you can plant containers in the spring, how long they will last in the fall, and whether you can leave them outside during the winter. See the map on page 151 of the appendix, or go to the "USDA Hardiness Zone Finder" at the National Gardening Association Web site, www.garden.org.

AHS heat zone ranges are listed in red. They indicate how well plants will fare during prolonged periods of hot weather. To find your heat zone, see the AHS heat zone map on page 150, or go to the "Heat Zone Finder" at the AHS Web site, www.ahs.org. Note: microclimates and local variables (such as soil type, pH, soil moisture levels, humidity, and wind exposure) can also affect hardiness.

Where light fertilization is indicated, apply half the manufacturer's recommended dose once every three weeks. For moderate fertilization, maintain a half dose but increase the frequency to once every two weeks. For containers that require heavy fertilization, opt for a half dose every week. See pages 136 to 141 for more on fertilizing.

In general, "recipes" are arranged by when the container display will be at its peak. Those at the beginning of the section will show early; those at the end will be at their best in the fall.

Full Sun

Tulips on Parade

Plant tulip bulbs in pots during the late fall and bring them outside the following spring. It's a great way to foil bulb-munching squirrels.

- 9 tulip bulbs *Tulipa* 'Double Early Monsella' (B) (3–8, 9–1)
- Potting mix, light fertilization, neutral pH
- 14-in.-dia. terra-cotta pot, 12-in. depth (min.)

Mix slow-release fertilizer with potting soil. Plant bulbs 6 inches deep, or about three times their diameter. Allow 3–4 inches between bulbs. Move pots to an unheated garage or shed for the winter. Water occasionally so the mix stays moist but not wet. Bring pots out to the porch or patio once leaves begin to emerge in the spring. Keep potting mix well watered. Double-early tulips bloom first, have rose-like double flowers, and are short stemmed—ideal for pots. The blooms are also longer lasting than many other tulips.

Full Sun to Partial Sun

Early Bloomers

The quickest way to put color where you want it in the spring is to head to the garden, spade in hand. Bring along a pot filled with a few inches of potting mix.

- Daffodils *Narcissus* (B) (3–9, 9–1)
- Potting mix, moderate fertilization
- 16-in.-dia. pot, 12-in. depth (min.)

Use your spade to cut a circle around a clump of daffodils, tulips, or whatever naturalized bulbs are emerging in your yard. Be sure the buds are showing. Pry up the clump, and place it in a container, without disturbing the roots. Fill around the edges with potting mix, and water. Make the transplant early so you can watch the plants grow. Blooms will last longer if kept out of direct sun. You can expect several weeks of show. When the blooms are done, carefully replant the clump in the ground.

Full Sun

Little Is Lovely

Early spring in many zones is all about diminutive blooms. Unfortunately, they are often hidden or go unseen. You can fix that by planting your favorite small flower bulbs in pots in the fall.

- 8 dwarf iris bulbs *Iris reticulata* 'Harmony' (B) (5–8, 8–5)
- 8 Greek windflowers *Anemone blanda* 'Blue Shades' (B) (4–8, 8–1)
- Potting mix, light fertilization, neutral to mildly acidic pH
- 12-in.-dia. pot or bowl, 6-in. depth (min.)

In the fall, in a shallow pot, plant dwarf iris bulbs 4 inches deep and Greek windflowers 3 inches deep. Try to space bulbs 2 to 3 inches apart. Dwarf iris bulbs are available in shades of blue, purple, and yellow. Greek windflowers come in white, pink, mauve, fuchsia, and blue. Move pots to an unheated garage or shed for the winter. Water occasionally so the mix stays moist but not wet. Bring pots out to the porch or patio early in the spring. Keep potting mix well watered.

Gardener's Tip

In the North, spring bulbs prefer full sun. In the South, for longer-lasting blooms, plant bulbs where there is partial sun.

Full Sun to Partial Sun

Growing Up Together

A terrific mid-spring combination mixes daffodils with hyacinths. Dry branches lend support to heavy blossoms.

- 8–12 hyacinths (half blue, half white) *Hyacinthus orientalis* (B) (5–9, 9–1)
- 8–12 daffodils *Narcissus* (B) (3–9, 9–1)
- Dry branches
- Potting mix, light fertilization, neutral pH
- Half-barrel planter

In the fall, layer bulbs in a large container, planting the daffodils 6 inches deep and the hyacinths 8 inches deep. Mulch heavily in colder zones to protect bulbs in winter, or move container to an unheated space.

Full Sun to Partial Sun

Spring Ahead!

Spring-blooming daffodils in a large whiskey barrel planter return year after year. The small-cupped *Narcissus* 'Geranium', shown, is white with an orange corona, or center. It is noted for having a lovely fragrance. Any daffodil may be substituted.

- 20–30 *Narcissus* 'Geranium' (B) (3–9, 9–1)
- Potting mix, light fertilization, neutral pH
- Half-barrel planter, 24-in. dia.

Mix a balanced time-release fertilizer with potting mix in a large container. Plant bulbs in fall to a depth of three times their diameter, usually about 6 inches. Mulch to protect bulbs in colder zones. Remove the mulch in early spring to make way for plants. Scratch a few tablespoons of bone meal into the potting mix surface. Mulch again as plants shrivel in warm weather to protect plants from overheating.

You cannot plan for the beautiful moment, but you can set the stage.

Combining Colors

Over the years, I've become convinced that color is largely a personal choice. Some gardeners prefer to create continual explosions of color throughout the season. Others prefer all white flowers or all foliage only. There are no wrong choices, but it's useful to know some basic rules of combining colors.

Hot colors, such as oranges and reds, are visually prominent. They will draw attention. Cool colors, such as blues and greens, are calming and tend to recede. Whites offer dazzling contrasts with foliage and glow in evening light for a lively, sophisticated effect.

Combinations that are commonly accepted as pleasing include those that are either complementary or analogous. Examples of complementary combinations include purples and yellows, and reds and greens. Examples of analogous combinations include oranges and yellows, and blues and greens.

In addition to hue, colors can be bright (intense) or pale. Mixing bright colors with pale colors is another way to create contrast.

When planning your color combinations, don't forget to consider the foliage colors of your selections. On one end of the spectrum are the purples and almost-blacks. On the other are whites and silvers. In between is almost every hue, including, of course, infinite shades of green.

Partial Sun to Shade

Coral and Cream

Simple is not only better; it can be exquisite, too. The interplay of similar leaf and petal shapes and analogous colors makes this arrangement by Kate Parisi extra special.

- 2 coral bells *Heuchera villosa* 'Creme Brulee', 'Caramel', or equivalent (P) (5–9, 9–1)
- 3 pansies *Viola:* any pale yellow cultivar (A) (9–1, NA)
- Potting mix, moderate fertilization, neutral pH
- 12-in. bowl or urn, 8-in. depth (min.)

Intersperse the coral bells with pale yellow pansies, allowing a few inches between plants. Place the urn directly in the garden to fill empty spots in spring, or use as a garden accent.

Circles and Shamrocks

Nasturtium and oxalis (wood sorrel) seem to defy gravity, with leaves balanced upon spaghetti-like stems. The former bloom profusely from late spring to fall. The latter may begin to fade if subject to too much sun.

- **2 purple shamrock *Oxalis triangularis* (B) [6–10, 1–9]**
- **4 nasturtium *Tropaeolum majus* color mix (P) [10–11, 12–1]**
- **Potting mix, moderate fertilization**
- **20-in.-dia. bowl, 7-in. depth (min.)**

Transplant small nasturtium and oxalis seedlings to container, or sow seeds and bulbs directly to a depth of 1 or 1½ inches. Space about 4 inches apart, with the shorter-habited oxalis nearest the pot rim. Flower petals and leaves are edible, but eat oxalis leaves only in small quantities.

Complementary Companions

On a color wheel, yellow is opposite purple, making the pair a complementary combination. Such contrasts are useful when creating eye-catching containers. Here the deep yellow of the coreopsis strongly contrasts with the purple of the salvia.

- **2 tickseed *Coreopsis auriculata* 'Zamphir' (P) [4–8, 9–1]**
- **3 sage *Salvia* 'East Friesland' (P) [4–8, 12–1]**
- **3 golden creeping Jenny *Lysimachia nummularia* (P) [4–8, 8–1]**
- **Potting mix, moderate fertilization, mildly acidic pH**
- **14-in.-dia. container, 8-in. depth (min.)**

Any combination of compact coreopsis and flowering salvia species will produce beautiful results. Plant the coreopsis in the center, salvia in the next orbit, and the creeping Jenny as a trailer near the container rim.

Gardener's Tip

By planting bulbs at varying depths, you can stagger their blooming period. The deeper you plant, the later the bloom. In mild-winter climates, you may also try refrigerating some of your bulbs for 6 to 8 weeks prior to planting. This will encourage them to bloom earlier in the season. Position late bloomers to the outside of the arrangement to hide spent flowers.

Partial Sun

Blades of Glory

Spiky plants are eye-catching because they contrast with more commonly found plant forms. Compound the contrast with the red, green, and black of this cordyline-iris-mondo grass trio, and use the container as an accent in a garden bed.

- 1 *Cordyline australis* 'Red Star' (8–11, 12–10)
- 2 *Iris variegata* (P) (3–9, 9–1)
- 2 black mondo grass *Ophiopogon planiscapus* 'Nigrescens' (P) (6–11, 12–1)
- Potting mix, moderate fertilization
- 14-in.-dia. container, 8-in. depth (min.)

Planted after the last frost date, the foliage reached 4 feet tall by mid-summer and was quite striking. Cordyline is not hardy in cold climates but may be brought indoors in winter and used as a houseplant. Eventually, it takes a tree-like form.

Many container gardens look too much like formal bouquets from a wedding. Allow room for the unexpected!

Full Sun to Partial Sun

Kate's Cosmos

To combine seven plant species (17 plants in all) in the same container requires a skilled hand. Here designer Kate Parisi achieves spectacular results.

- 3 *Cosmos bipinnatus* 'Sonata White' or similar (A) (NA, 12–1)
- 2 *Dichondra argentea* 'Silver Falls' (P) (10–12, 12–9)
- 1 New Zealand flax *Phormium:* any tall, red or bronze cultivar, such as 'Evening Glow' or 'Dusky Chief' (P) (9–11, 12–2)
- 3 *Petunia:* any cream or white trailing variety, such as 'Shock Wave Ivory' or 'Easy Wave White' (A) (NA, 12–1)
- 3 country borage or spurflower *Plectranthus amboinicus* (P) (9–11, 12–1)
- 3 fan flower *Scaevola aemula* 'Purple Fanfare' (P) (9–12, 12–1)
- 2 red sweet potato vine *Ipomoea batatas:* any variety, such as 'Carolina Red' or 'Blackie' (V) (10–11, 12–1)
- Potting mix, moderate fertilization, neutral pH
- 24- to 30-in.-dia. urn, 20-in. depth (min.)

Plant the flax in the center of the urn, and position the cosmos plants around it, a few inches away. In the next orbit, alternately plant the spurflower, petunias, and fan flower. Plant the red sweet potato vine and the dichondra around the urn perimeter. Fertilize with a complete water-soluble fertilizer every week while watering.

Avoiding the Predictable

Kate Parisi studied flower arranging at the Constance Spry Flower School in London and employs many of the same principles in her container gardens. In addition to the container recipe above, she contributed the arrangements on pages 84 and 88. Parisi, who is also an accomplished jewelry designer, often gets her inspiration from nature. She prefers a little unruliness to arrangements that are regular and formal.

"I like to see how the containers will evolve," she says. "If something isn't working, I'll pull it out and replace it with something else."

Parisi adds interest to containers by using contrast: broad leaves behind small ones; big blossoms mixed with tiny ones; glowing yellow-green leaves and deep reds cohabiting with everyday greens.

Parisi uses all sorts of plants in her ornamental arrangements, including edibles such as kale, lettuce, thyme, and Swiss chard. Some of her favorite ornamentals include plants you may never have known, such as plectranthus. Its broad, fuzzy, pale green leaves add body and a lush texture to Parisi's arrangements. Scaevola, with its barbed-leaf edges and fan-like clusters of starburst blossoms, contrasts nicely with tamer-looking plants. Her other selections include favorites, such as sweet potato vine, petunias, and lantana.

Parisi likes to use colors in her containers that are similar to those found in the gardens that surround her contain-ers. The potato vine and New Zealand flax in the urn opposite, for example, pick up the hues of Joe Pye weed, penstemon Husker Red, and Sand cherry planted in nearby beds. Similarly, the dichondra and plectranthus echo a nearby patch of lamb's ear. In this way, her garden-sited containers don't look out of place.

Parisi's containers tend to be playful and riotous. There's something new to look at nearly every time you walk by them. She does not, however, rely on flowers alone to achieve her results.

"They're important, of course," she says, "but I probably like the foliage of plants better than the flowers."

Full Sun to Partial Sun

Blues Festival

This old stone trough comes alive with a selection of blues and purples from Proven Winners, a national plant supplier.

- 1 snapdragon *Angelonia* 'Angelface Blue' (P) (9–10, 10–9)
- 2 *Calibrachoa* 'Trailing Blue' Super Bells series (P) (9–11, 12–1)
- 1 baby's breath, *Gypsophila*, 'Festival Star' (P) (5–9, 9–1)
- 1 licorice plant *Helichrysum petiolare* 'Limelight' (P) (9–11, 12–1)
- 1 *Nemesia fruticans* 'Bluebird' (P) (9–11, NA)
- 1 *Petunia* 'Supertunia Mini Blue Veined' Supertunia series (P) (9–15, 12–1)
- Potting mix, moderate fertilization, mildly acidic pH
- 6-in. x 24-in. trough, 6-in. depth (min.)

In the back of the container, plant two rows of the petunia in left corner, snapdragon and gypsophila in the center, and one calibrachoa in the right corner. In the front row, plant one calibrachoa in the left corner, the nemesia front and center, and the licorice plant in the right corner. Apply water-soluble fertilizer twice a month at half dose.

Partial Sun

Old-Fashioned Favorites

This classic arrangement mixes updated versions of old-fashioned flowers for spring- and summer-long blossoms. Persian shield and sweet potato vine provide the contrast—and the pop.

- 2 sweet potato vines *Ipomoea batatas* 'Margarita' (V) (10–11, 12–1)
- 2 flossflowers *Ageratum* 'Artist's Purple' Artist series (P) (10–13, 12–1)
- 1 *Petunia* 'Supertunia Mini Strawberry Pink Veined' Supertunia series (P) (9–15, 12–1)
- 1 *Verbena* hybrid 'Superbena Burgundy' Superbena series (P) (8–15, 12–1)
- 1 Persian shield *Strobilanthes dyerianus* (S) (10–12, 12–1)
- Potting mix, moderate fertilization, mildly acidic pH
- 14-in.-dia. pot, 12-in. depth (min.)

Plant the Persian shield at the back of the pot. Put the ageratum on one side and the verbena on the other. Plant the petunia and the sweet potato vine to the front.

Full Sun to Partial Sun

Dutch Treat

Ornamental containers don't need to be large to be admired. Sometimes it's the little touches that catch the eye, according to designer Marilyn Thorkilsen. Nearly everyone who passes her Dutch shoe planters, for example, can't help but stop and smile.

- 2 ruptureworts *Hernaria glabra* 'Sea Foam' (P) (7–12, 12–10)
- 2 clusters of hens and Chicks *Sempervivum x barbulatum* from Valle Quarozzo (C) (4–8, 8–1)
- Potting mix, moderate fertilization, mildly acidic pH
- Old shoes or shoe-shaped planter

Partially fill the shoe planter with potting soil, and plant the rupturewort as the laces. Plant the hens and chicks hybrid near the heel. This planter did not have drain holes, so it required extra care to avoid overwatering. You may control watering by placing such planters under an eave or porch roof.

Full Sun to Partial Sun

Spring Frolic

Rosemary provides the height, and silver thyme adds contrast next to the the violas and lobelia. Later in the season, designer Marilyn Thorkilsen replaces the violas with evolvulus (*Evolvulus glomeratus* 'Blue Daze').

- 2 thyme *Thymus* 'Hartington Silver' (H) (NA, 12–1)
- 2 *Viola*, any blue variety (P) (6–8, 8–6)
- 3 pansies *Viola x wittrockiana* 'Karma Purple' Karma series (P) (NA, 9–1)
- 1 rosemary *Rosmarinus officinalis* (S) (8–11, 12–8)
- 2 *Lobelia erinus* 'Riviera Marine Blue' (P) (8–11, 8–1)
- Potting mix, moderate fertilization, neutral pH
- 16-in.-dia. concrete urn, 12-in. depth (min.)

Plant the rosemary in the center, and then surround it with violas (vary the colors from blue to purple for added interest), lobelia, and silver thyme. This urn was planted in the following order, clockwise from the front: silver thyme, lobelia, blue violas, silver thyme, purple violas, lobelia, and purple violas.

Partial Sun to Shade

Show Stopper

With more than 1,500 species, you have many begonias from which to choose. For containers, I prefer the tuberous type for their mass and their ability to provide colorful blossoms in shade.

- **4 *Begonia tuberhybrida* group 'Non-Stop Apricot' (or preferred color) (B) (9–15, 9–1)**
- **Potting mix, light fertilization**
- **7-in. x 30-in. trough, 7-in. depth**
- **10-in. stakes**

Remove tubers from packing material carefully to avoid damaging small sprouts. Plant right side up in a small container. Cover tuber with more potting mix, and water thoroughly. The top of the root ball should be about 1 inch below the pot rim. Transplant to a larger container when the plant is a few inches tall, and move the container outside after the danger of frost has passed. Fertilize every two weeks with a water-soluble fertilizer.

Full Sun to Partial Sun

Two Ways to Use Calla Lilies

Calla lilies are beautiful enough to plant solo, as shown at right (*Zantedeschia* 'Hotshot'). You can also try pairing them with licorice plant (above).

- **3 licorice plants *Helichrysum petiolare* 'Limelight' (P) (9–11, 12–1)**
- **1 calla lily *Zantedeschia* 'Butterscotch' or 'Bridal Bliss' (B) (8–10, 10–1)**
- **1 *Begonia Tuberhybrida* group 'Non-Stop Apple Blossom' (partly hidden) (B) (9–15, 9–1)**
- **Potting mix, light fertilization, mildly acidic pH**
- **20-in.-dia. basket or pot, 12-in. depth**

Plant calla lily and begonia in the center. Surround with licorice plants.

Full Sun to Partial Sun

Dazzler

Roses tend to be labor intensive, but not this one from Proven Winners. It blooms all summer and is disease resistant. No spraying necessary.

- Rose *Rosa* 'Hormeteorie' Oso Easy series, Strawberry Crush (4–9, 10–1)
- Potting mix, moderate fertilization, mildly acidic pH
- 14-in. pot or urn, 12-in. depth

Mix a time-release fertilizer in potting mix, and plant in early summer. Fertilize weekly to increase blooming with a water-soluble product. Look for fertilizers that have low nitrogen percentages. Large, double blossoms turn from pink to cream.

Non-Stop Blossoms

New Guinea impatiens are perhaps the lowest maintenance plant in my garden. In a deep hanging basket in shade, they can go without watering for a couple of days, need little fertilizer, and require no deadheading.

- **New Guinea impatiens *Impatiens* 'Balcebpiel' Celebrette series (P) (9–15, 12–1)**
- **Sphagnum moss *Sphagnum cymbifolium* (P) (NA, NA)**
- **Potting mix, light fertilization**
- **Wire basket, 12-in. dia., 12-in. depth**

Plant around the time azaleas bloom. Keep moss green through spring and early summer by spraying it when you water the container.

Miniature Hosta

Miniature versions of plants you have in your yard make especially good accents on a deck or patio. 'Blue Moon' hosta and other small-to-medium species look great in containers and are quite well behaved.

- **1 *Hosta* 'Blue Moon' (P) or similar (3–8, 9–2)**
- **Sphagnum moss *Sphagnum cymbifolium* (P) (NA, NA)**
- **Potting mix, light fertilization, neutral pH**
- **8-in.-dia. basket, 6-in. depth (min.)**

Plant in a basket or other small container, and use live sphagnum moss as a mulch. This can withstand partial sun but, like most hostas, prefers shade. Small, white, bell-shaped flowers appear in midsummer. Hosta (along with daylilies and sedum autumn joy) will survive winters outside in containers.

Lining a Basket with Moss

1 Live sphagnum moss, available from florists or by mail, comes in sections that are roughly 1 or 2 sq. ft. Keep cool and moist until you can use it.

2 Press a large section of moss over the basket bottom, root side up.

3 Build up the sides by fitting in additional pieces of moss.

4 Add potting mix until the container is about half full.

5 Press the potting mix against the root side of the moss to hold it in place. You may plant now or later.

6 Add potting mix as needed, and trim off excess moss at rim. Note: keep sphagnum moss moist, or it will turn brown. Mine survived the summer in a shady place.

Needles and Pins

Combine plants with different foliage but similar textures or markings to create entertaining containers. The viewer's enjoyment comes from discovering similarities that are not immediately apparent.

- 1 coral bell *Heuchera* 'Green Spice' or similar veining (P) [4–9, 9–1]
- 1 compact heavenly bamboo *Nandina domestica* 'Compacta' (T) [6–9, 12–4]
- 1 rock stonecrop *Sedum reflexum* 'Angelina' (C) [3–9, 7–3]
- Potting mix, light fertilization
- 12-in.-dia. pot, 12-in. depth (min.)

Plant stonecrop to the back, coral bell to the front, and the bamboo in the center. For large troughs, repeat every 10 inches.

Hen House

Strawberry pots are a great way to display succulents. In this pot by container garden designer Ruth Zelig, the corkscrew rush provides the contrast—and the fun!

- 2 corkscrew rush *Juncus effusus spiralis* 'Unicorn' (P) [5–9, 9–6]
- 2 Irish moss *Sagina subulata* 'Aurea' (P) [4–7, 7–1]
- 3 clusters of hens and chicks *Sempervivum tectorum* (C) [4–8, 8–1]
- 3 rock stonecrop *Sedum reflexum* 'Angelina' (C) [3–9, 7–3]
- Potting mix with sand mixed in, light fertilization, neutral pH
- Large strawberry pot with 5 or 6 large openings

Mix potting soil with 10 percent sand for improved drainage. Fill the pot to the first openings with potting mix, and plant hens and chicks, and stonecrop. Continue to fill and plant, pressing the mix firmly around the roots. Save the Irish moss for the topmost opening to better show its cascading effect. Plant corkscrew rush at the jar top.

Gardener's Tip

Many perennials will not look their best in a container during the first season. Peonies and astilbes, for example, take more than a year to get well established in a container. Keep such containers in the background this year—and reap the rewards next year.

Full Sun to Partial Sun

Dahlia and the Dragon

Containers allow the outlandish. Here pretty dahlias get cozy with sumptuous coleus. Notice how the petals of the former echo the leaf edge's shape of the latter. The chameleon plant (bottom left) mirrors the coleus markings and contributes a peppery orange scent.

- 2 coleus *Solenostemon scutellariodes* 'Dragon Black' or 'Florida Sun Rose' (P) (10–12, 12–1)
- 3 *Dahlia* 'Eye Candy' or any compact dahlia cultivar (B) (8–11, 12–1)
- 2 chameleon plant *Houttuynia cordata* 'Chameleon' (P) (5–11, 12–1)
- Potting mix, moderate fertilization
- 14-in.-dia. pot, 12-in. depth (min.)

In late spring, or when soil temperature reaches 60° F, plant dahlia bulbs at the back of the pot, coleus seedlings in the center, and the chameleon plant seedlings to the front so they receive some shade from the coleus.

Partial Sun to Shade

Hosta Hosts Asian Lily

This two-plant container couples an unlikely duo for a long-lasting, ever-changing display. See the foliage unfurl through the spring. Then watch as the lilies bloom in early summer and the hosta blooms midsummer. The lily foliage will wither and need to be clipped, but the hosta foliage will look good through the fall.

- 3 *Hosta* 'Abby Plantain Lily' (P) (3–9, 9–2)
- 5 Asian lily *Lilium* 'Souvenir' or similar (B) (8–1, 4–8)
- Potting mix, light fertilization
- 16-in.-dia. pot, 12-in. depth (min.)

Plant emerging hosta plants or roots and lily bulbs in spring to a depth of 6 to 8 inches. I replant the hosta in the ground in October and save the lily bulbs in a dry cool place for the following year.

Partial Sun

Terrific Trailers

Mix showy caladium with trailers for a gracious effect.

- 1 Persian shield *Strobilanthes dyerianus* (S) (10–12, 12–1)
- 3 *Caladium* 'Aaron', 'Berry Patch', or similar (B) (10–15, 12–4)
- 2 licorice plants *Helichrysum petiolare* 'Limelight' (P) (9–11, 12–1)
- 3 *Impatiens walleriana* (trailing variety) (P) (10–15, 12–1)
- Potting mix, light fertilization
- Window box, 6 x 24 x 7 in. deep

Plant caladium bulbs along the back and Persian shield in either back corner. Alternate the trailing impatiens and licorice plants along the front.

Gardener's Tip

Many houseplants do well outdoors during the summer. You may even mix them with outdoor plants in containers. Most will prefer shade or partial shade. Acclimate them by first moving them to a shady spot.

Planting Surprises

aster gardener Ruth Zelig, a container-garden designer from New Jersey, reminds her clients that her designs are not static—they're meant to change throughout the season or seasons. In fact, Zelig often includes little surprises in her containers, such as bulbs that don't show up for several weeks or more. Her favorites include caladium, crocosmia, day lilies, and elephant ears. For the latter, she prefers the small Black Magic cultivar (*Colocasia esculenta*).

If you do plant summer bulbs in your containers, Zelig suggests inserting a labeled marker stick to remind yourself where you planted the bulb. She also adds seeds to create surprises. The seeds must be fast-growing and not too fussy. Nasturtium, alyssum, and lobelia are a few of her favorites. Of course, any combination of tuber, bulb, or rhizome and annuals will create continual change. For example, plant a container of pansies at the first sign of spring, but intersperse several varieties of dwarf hosta roots and ferns that can take over when the pansies begin to fade.

Partial Sun to Shade

Rhapsody in Red

One of several designs from Pacific Northwest designers Joanna Guzzetta and Jennifer Williams, this container employs both color and textural contrasts. Their secret: pick a theme and stick to it. In this case, it's the red-green contrasts.

- 2 elephant ear *Colocasia esculenta* 'Illustris' (B) (8–15, 12–7)
- 2 Chinese plumbago *Cerotostigma willmottianum* 'My Love' (S) (6–9, 9–6)
- 1 alumroot *Heuchera* 'Berry Smoothy' (P) (3–8, 9–1)
- 2 coleus *Solenostemon scutellarioides* 'Lifelime' (P) (10–12, 12–1)
- 1 coleus *Solenostemon scutellarioides* 'Big Red' (P) (10–12, 12–1)
- 1 *Ajuga reptans* 'Black Scallop' (P) (3–9, 9–1)
- Potting mix, moderate fertilization
- 16-in. bowl or urn, 12-in. depth (min.)

Plant the elephant ear to the rear and the two varieties of coleus to the center. Plant the alumroot, plumbago (which will turn red in fall), and the ajuga to the front.

Made in the Shade

Kate Parisi converted her spring pot of violas and coral bells (page 69) to a summer shade container by removing the violas, digging hosta and fern from her garden, and combining them with a begonia.

- 2 *Hosta,* any compact species
- 1 fern, any compact species
- 1 *Begonia semperflorens* 'Nightlife Red' (P) [13–15, 12–1]
- 2 coral bells *Heuchera villosa* 'Creme Brulee', 'Caramel', or similar (P) [5–9, 9–1]
- Potting mix, moderate fertilization
- 12-in. bowl or urn, 8-in. depth (min.)

Plant the begonia as close to the center as possible. Surround with the fern and hosta plants. Choose a compact hosta so it doesn't overwhelm the pot.

Fern Depot

Ferns are intriguing. Unfortunately, they're often overlooked in the garden—especially small species. A container—this one was placed on a stone—is all it takes to draw attention to them.

- 2 Japanese painted fern *Athyrium niponicum* 'Pewter Lace' or 'Burgundy Lace' (P) [5–8, 8–1]
- 1 eastern marsh fern *Thelypteris palustris* or similar (P) [3–9, 9–1]
- Moss collected from yard
- Potting mix with 10 percent sand, mildly acidic pH
- 12-in.-dia., 6-in. depth (min.) hypertufa container

Combine sand and potting mix with a slow-release fertilizer that has high nitrogen content. Plant fern roots or young plants in early spring. Add moss if available. At the end of the season, replant ferns in the ground.

Gardener's Tip

Don't limit yourself to planting annuals in your containers. Perennials often produce distinctive displays and come back year after year. Planting perennials is also less costly. Simply split perennials in your yard, and move them to containers. Be sure that you pry gently when disentangling roots to avoid harming the plant.

Full Sun to Partial Sun

Flaunt Your Flutes

Sometimes all it takes is one plant in the right pot, as with this container from Ruth Zelig. Notice how the shape of the leaves mimics the fluted rim of the pot.

- 1 *Geranium stellar pelargonium 'Vancouver Centennial'* (P) (12–15, 12–1)
- Potting mix: moderate fertilization
- 10-in.-dia. ornamental container, 8-in. depth (min.)

Plant this geranium in late spring, and fertilize every two or three weeks with a water-soluble fertilizer while watering. Deadhead regularly, and over-winter indoors.

Shining Star

The festive pinwheel patterns of the phlox combined with white trailing petunias will light the way to your door.

- **3** *Petunia* **'Supertunia White' Supertunia series (P) [9–15, 12–1]**
- **3** *Phlox hybrid* **'Intensia Star Brite' Intensia series [A] [NA, 12–1]**
- **Potting mix, moderate fertilization**
- **14-in.-dia. basket**

Plant the phlox and the petunias in an alternating pattern, leaving 3 or 4 inches in all directions. Both plants will bloom profusely throughout the summer.

Low-Maintenance Charmer

If you're a beginner, this is a good two-species arrangement with which to get started. Both species are vigorous drought- and disease-resistant growers.

- **2 sweet potato vine** *Ipomoea batatas* **'Margarita' [V] [10–11, 12–1]**
- **2** *Petunia hybrid* **'Lemon Plume' Supertunia series [A] [10–11, 12–1]**
- **Potting mix, light fertilization, mildly acidic pH**
- **10-in.-dia. urn, 8-in. depth [min.]**

Plant the petunia to one side of an urn and the sweet potato vine to the other. Fertilize once every two weeks while watering, with a water-soluble product. This arrangement is low maintenance and will show well from spring to fall. It also works nicely in baskets and window boxes. The chartreuse mass of sweet potato vine, accentuated with the yellow petunia blossoms, stands out almost anywhere, but a dark background will make them pop.

Partial Sun

Layer Cake

The trick to creating the layered effect is to plant in rows. Position the taller species at the back and the shorter ones at the front. This assumes a container that you'll view from one direction.

- 2 umbrella plant *Cyperus involucratus* (P) (10–11, 12–7)
- 3 African daisy *Osteospermum hybrid* 'Soprano Purple' (P) (9–11, 6–1)
- 3 *Euphorbia hypericifolia* 'Inneuphdia' Diamond Frost series (P) (9–11, NA)
- 5 oxalis bulbs *Oxalis crassipes* 'Garden Hardy Pink' (B) (5–10, NA)
- Potting mix: moderate fertilization
- 18-in.-dia. concrete pot or urn, 12-in. depth (min.)

Mix a slow-release fertilizer with your potting mix. Place umbrella plant in the back of the pot, 4 inches from the rim. In the center, plant the African daisy. A few inches from the front rim, plant the oxalis and euphorbia. Encourage the latter to send some shoots to peek from above the African daisy. Note: umbrella plants like wet roots.

Full Sun

Some Like It Hot

When other container plants wilt, this one will continue to produce its tufted yellow flowers from summer through fall. Its foliage is silvery green, and it reaches an 8- to 14-inch height and a 2- to 3-foot width.

- 1 strawflower *Chrysocephalum apiculatum* 'Flambe Yellow' (P) (9–10, 12–1)
- Potting mix, moderate fertilization
- 10-in. pot, 8-in. depth (min.)

Plant as a single-species container, or mix with other sun-loving plants, such as phlox hybrid 'Intensia White'. This strawflower is heat and drought tolerant.

Full Sun to Partial Sun

Cutting Zinnias

A grouping of zinnias on a deck or patio provides a beautiful display of color that lasts from mid-summer to fall. This heirloom variety grows to 3 feet and is great for cuttings. The long-lasting blooms, which are 3–4 inches in diameter, fade from red to dusty pink.

- 5 *Zinnia* 'Exquisite' (A) (NA, 12–1)
- Potting mix, moderate fertilization
- 12-in. pot, 10-in. depth (min.)
- Stakes (when necessary)

Start from seed in early March and transplant to larger pots in mid-April. Bring outdoors after danger of frost has passed, and transplant once more to an outdoor pot or trough. Note: if not needed for cutting, you may want to try a shorter species. *Zinnia elegans* (State Fair series) grow to 1 or 2 feet and have similar blossoms.

Full Sun to Partial Sun

Lantana x 2

Lantana can be used alone (right) or in combination (above) for stunning displays as the weather warms.

- 3 nasturtium *Tropaeolum majus* Alaska series (P) (10–11, 12–1)
- 3 *Lantana camara* 'Balucrehot' Lucky series (right) and *Lantana camara* 'Balucwite' (above) (P) (10–11, 12–4)
- 1 New Zealand flax *Phormium* any tall, red, or bronze cultivar, such as 'Evening Glow' or 'Dusky Chief' (P) (9–11, 12–2)
- Potting mix, light fertilization, mildly acidic pH
- 12-in.-dia. pot or urn

For the container above, plant flax in the center and surround with lantana and nasturtium, alternating placement.

Beautiful Visitors

It seems that all the world is in love with butterflies and hummingbirds—and I'm no exception. To lure them to your container garden, plant the things they like.

Butterflies are attracted to most colors and prefer daisy-type blooms, such as coneflowers. Clusters of zinnias, marigolds, and verbenas work, too. If you want to attract egg-laying butterflies so that you can witness their life cycle, grow the host plants they prefer. For monarchs, put milkweed in one of your mixed containers. For the black swallowtail, plant curly parsley, dill, fennel, or carrots. Yes, the caterpillars will do some chewing on your host plants, but the show is worth the price. For a list of butterfly host plants, visit www.thebutterflysite.com.

Hummingbirds are also attracted to color, especially red. Butterfly bush, rose of Sharon, flowering quince, and honeysuckle will all draw hummingbirds but tend to be ungainly in containers. My preferences tend toward the more manageable bee balm, begonia, columbine, fuchsia, impatiens, and salvia. For more butterfly- and hummingbird-friendly plants, see the "recipes" on this page and opposite.

Full Sun to Partial Sun

Butterfly Magnet

You can use new compact varieties of butterfly bush in containers. This one produces long abundant blossom clusters.

- 1 butterfly bush *Buddelia davidii* 'Peacock' English Butterfly series (S) [5–9, 9–2]
- 2 wood spurge *Euphorbia hybrid* 'Kalipso' (P) [6–9, 9–2]
- 1 *Euphorbia hypericifolia* 'Inneuphdia' Diamond Frost series (P) [9–11, NA]
- 2 coleus *Solenostemon scutellariodes* 'Merlin's Magic' (P) [10–11, 12–1]
- 2 betony *Stachys* 'Sentimental Journey' (P) [10–11, NA]
- Potting mix, moderate fertilization, mildly acidic pH
- 20-in.-dia. bowl or urn, 18-in depth (mln.)

Plant the butterfly bush at the back of the container. Plant the coleus in front of it, in the center. The euphorbia go to the right and left. Plant the betony to the front so it will trail over the rim. Prune the butterfly bush as needed.

Full Sun to Partial Sun

Fourth of July

Set off your own "flower" works next Independence Day by planting this pretty red, white, and blue summer mix.

- 3 *Petunia* 'Supertunia White' Supertunia series (P) [9–15, 12–1]
- 2 Marguerite Daisy *Argyranthemum frutescens* 'Helio White' Molimba series (P) [10–11, 12–1]
- 2 *Nemesia* 'Cranberry' Sunsatia series (P) [10–11, NA]
- 2 *Verbena hybrid* 'Babylon Blue' and 2 'Babylon Red' Babylon series (A) [8–11, NA]
- Potting mix, light fertilization
- 30-in. window basket or trough

In the back row, plant the nemesia in the corners and the Marguerite daisies between them. In the front row, left to right, plant the red verbena, petunias, blue verbena, petunias, and red verbena. Every two weeks apply a water-soluble fertilizer while watering.

Full Sun to Partial Sun

Heavenly Orb

With many hanging baskets, you see more container than plant. Not so with this creation from Proven Winners.

- 1 *Petunia* 'Supertunia Mini Blue Veined' Supertunia series (P) [9–15, 12–1]
- 2 *Petunia* 'Supertunia Royal Velvet' Supertunia series (P) [9–15, 12–1]
- 1 *Verbena* 'Superbena Large Lilac Blue' Superbena series (P) [8–15, 12–1]
- Potting mix, light fertilization
- 16-in.-dia. hanging basket

In compass fashion, plant the verbena in the "north" position, a few inches from the rim. Plant the Royal Velvet petunias in the south position. Plant the Mini Blue Veined petunia to the east and the remaining Royal Velvet petunia to the west.

Petunias are one of the more versatile plants in the garden. They can be used as fillers, spillers, and even as thrillers.

Full Sun to Partial Sun

Standing Tall

This small urn is elevated several feet with a brick base. The cloud of bacopa it contains makes Jackie Heller's backyard garden feel magical.

- 4 bacopa *Sutera cordata* 'Giant Snowflake' (P) (8–10, 12–10)
- 2 *Petunia* 'Mini Rose Veined' Supertunia series (P) (9–15, 12–1)
- 2 *Petunia* 'Surfinia Purple' Surfinia series (P) (9–15, 12–1)
- 2 *Calibrachoa hybrid* 'Superbells Rose' Superbells series (P) (9–11, 12–1)
- Potting mix, light fertilization, mildly acidic
- 12-in.-dia. urn or pot, 10-in. depth (min.)

Plant the veined petunias in the center of the urn. Surround them with the purple petunias and the rose calibrachoa. Fill open spots with the bacopa.

Summer Fountain

Open-form plants, such as fountain grass, reflect sunlight in amazing ways, catching the eye quicker than even the brightest flower.

- 3 *Calibrachoa* 'Superbells Peach' Superbells series (P) (9–11, 12–1)
- 2 coleus *Solenostemon scutellarioides* 'Sedona' (P) (10–12, 12–1)
- 1 purple fountain grass *Pennisetum sctaceum* (P) (8–11, 12–8)
- Potting mix, moderate fertilization
- 12-in.-dia. pot, 10-in. depth (min.)

Plant the calibrachoa seedlings along the front rim. Plant the two coleus in the center. Plant the fountain grass to the back.

Simply Succulent

Succulents come in many shapes and hues. This collection from Portland, Oregon, designers Joanna Guzzetta and Jennifer Williams can grow just about anywhere but prefer dry conditions. Overwatering will induce root rot.

- 1 *Aloe vera* (C) (10–15, 12–10)
- 2 livingstone daisy *Dorotheanthus bellidiformis* 'Mezoo Trailing Red' (A) (10–15, 9–1)
- 3 sedum blue carpet *Sedum hispanicum minus* 'Purple Form' (P) (4–8, 9–1)
- 2 pork and beans *Sedum rubrotinctum* (C) (9–11, 10–9)
- 3 paddle plant *Kalanchoe thyrsiflora* (C) (11–15, 12–1)
- 1 *Mandevilla hybrid* 'Audrey' (V) (9–11, 12–1)
- 1 *Echeveria* 'Black Prince' (C) (NA, NA)
- Potting mix with sand mixed in, light fertilization
- 14-in.-dia. ceramic or terra-cotta pot, 12-in. depth (min.)

Place the aloe to the rear of the pot. Place the paddle plants and the mandevilla vine in the center, 4 or 5 inches apart. Alternately place the sedums and livingstone daisy plants along the front, leaving an opening for the echeveria. Water succulents once a week during hot weather and once every few weeks during cooler months.

Nonplant Objects

N early any container garden benefits from nonplant materials and objects. Interesting stones immediately come to mind. So do the gravel and sand expanses of dry Japanese gardens. Many other objects can find a place and role in your creation. I enjoy copper gazing globes, or gazing balls, which shine in winter and get overgrown in summer. Consider the use of lanterns, wind chimes, armillaries, plaques, statues, fountains, and birdbaths. Such objects become the punctuation of a garden, helping to direct the viewer's gaze or to separate one "thought" from another. Found objects can serve the same purpose. Once you begin to plan a container "garden," you'll find yourself keeping your eyes peeled for driftwood, shells, and architectural artifacts, such as pillars and corbels.

Partial Sun

Light My Fire

Feel the heat with this fire-like combo from designers Joanna Guzzetta and Jennifer Williams. The secret to their success: pick a theme and stick to it. Choosing the perfect container also helps!

- 2 creeping Jenny *Lysimachia congestiflora* 'Persian Chocolate' (P) (5–10, 9–6)
- 3 coleus *Solenostemon scutellariodes* 'Roaring Fire' (P) (10–12, 12–1)
- 3 *Verbena* 'Flamenco Scarlet' (A) (8–11, NA)
- Potting mix, moderate fertililization
- 14-in. x 14-in. ceramic container, 12-in. depth (min.)

Plant the coleus at the back of the pot. Plant the creeping Jenny to the sides, and plant the verbena in the front. The coleus and creeping Jenny are not fussy about exposure, but turn the pot so the verbena gets as much sun as possible.

Reflective elements can enhance a container garden. Old mirrors, gazing globes, birdbaths, and small pools of water can all add depth and intrigue to your creation.

Full Sun to Partial Sun

Holiday Welcome

Don't leave your favorite urn empty during the holidays. Fill it with fruits and cuttings, as designer Marilyn Thorkilsen did here.

- Fruits, such as pineapple, apples, and oranges
- Ornamental leaves, such as magnolia
- Cuttings, such as spruce, pine, and holly boughs
- Bowl, urn on pedestal

Remove old plants, but leave potting mix in place. Invert the bowl, and set it on the potting mix. Place pineapple on the bowl, and surround it with oranges, leaves, and boughs. Bring fruits inside in freezing weather.

Full Sun to Partial Sun

Autumn Sunshine

Tired of the traditional fall mums and millet? Try this Proven Winners combo (above) to brighten a fall day. It will stand up to cold temperatures, up until there is a hard frost.

- 2 *Calibrachoa* 'Superbells Yellow Chiffon' Superbells series (P) (9–11, 12–1)
- 1 Marguerite daisy *Argyranthemum frutescens* 'Butterfly' (P) (10–11, 12–1)
- 2 coral bells *Heuchera villosa* 'Licorice' Dolce series or similar (P) (4–9, 9–1)
- 2 creeping wire vine *Muehlenbeckia* (V) (8–10, 10–8)
- Potting mix, moderate fertilization
- 12-in.-dia. pot, 10-in. depth (min.)

Plant the Marguerite daisies in the back. Use more than one plant in a larger pot. Plant the coral bells to the sides, right and left. Plant the calibrachoa in the center. Fill empty areas along the rim with the wire vine.

Chapter 5

Herbs and Vegetables

For "earth-bound" gardeners it may be hard to believe, but just about any edible you can grow in the ground can be grown in a container sitting on your deck or patio. Would you believe that you can produce 20 ears of corn in a 30-inch trough? Or 6 pounds of tomatoes in a 16-inch-diameter clay pot? And with herbs costing $10 to $15 per pound in the supermarket, even just a few potted favorites will quickly pay for themselves.

o keep my edible plant containers colorful, I enjoy combining vegetables and herbs with colorful annuals. Nasturtiums, for example, dress up just about any container, and as a bonus, the leaves and blossoms may be eaten. I also like mixing vegetable plants with herbs. Bush beans and rosemary, and lettuce and sage are two good combos. Better yet, they are considered "companion plantings"—plants that in some way benefit each other.

Whether you're planning a small edibles patch on the deck or a container garden that's big enough to feed your family, success begins with choosing quality seeds and healthy plants. A good indication of seed quality is how much information the seed company puts on the package. Look for seed count, packaging date, sell-by date, germi-

nation temperature, days to germination, germination rate, days to maturity, planting depth and spacing, and special requirements. Some seeds, for example, need light to germinate; others prefer total darkness. Some seeds must be nicked or "scarified"; others must be soaked or exposed to cold temperatures for a period of time. Another good indication of quality is whether the company guarantees its seeds.

Buying healthy vegetable and herb seedlings is the same as buying annuals. (See page 57.) In addition, avoid pots with overcrowded seedlings. Not only will they be less healthy, but they will be tough to separate. As with all container plantings, choose varieties that can be planted close together and that have compact habits.

Gardener's Tip

The bigger the seed, the easier it will be to start at home. I start
my tomatoes, eggplants, peppers, and basil from seed but prefer
to buy plants when it comes to dill, oregano, rosemary, and thyme.
The same goes for flowers. Large-seed species, such as
nasturtium or moon flowers, are easy to start. Coleus, with its
small seeds, is more difficult.

Starting Plants from Seed

When the winter seems exceptionally long, which it often does here in New England, I enjoy starting my vegetable (and flowering) plants from seed. In addition to giving me a sneak preview of spring, doing so allows me to choose from a much wider variety of plants than I'd find at the local nursery.

Seedlings will need 12 to 16 hours of light daily in order to be strong and healthy. For gardeners in northern zones, this means you'll need to set up a seedling nursery under fluorescent lights. I built mine from scrap wood. A pair of 4-foot-long fixtures fitted with a mix of warm and cool bulbs supply the light. You may also use full-spectrum bulbs, but be ready to spend more. An adjustable shelf allows me to keep the plants within a few inches of the lights after germination—and to lower the seed trays as the plants grow.

Each peat tray (left) has 50 2-in. cells. Two of these trays are more than enough for most container gardeners. I use mine to grow a mix of vegetables and flowering plants.

Make a diagram (below) of your trays so you know what is planted where. Keep trays warm and moist but not soggy. You may water with a spray bottle at first.

Starting vegetable plants from seed is best done in trays of small peat cells. They are often sold with a plastic tray that catches excess water and a clear lid that's useful for keeping the mix warm while seeds are germinating. Remove the lid once the seeds have germinated.

I prefer to fill the cells with a fine-texture potting mix that includes a bit of fertilizer rather than a seed-starting mix because this gives seedlings more growing time before I have to transplant them. When the seedlings have fully developed "adult" leaves (usually the leaves that appear after the first pair), I transplant the healthiest ones to bigger peat pots—or whatever I can find, including paper cups with holes punched in the bottom. This, of course, means there may not be enough room under the lights for all the seedlings. Place the extras at sunny windows, or set up additional lights.

When starting seeds indoors, schedule your sowing carefully. Some plants will be ready for transplanting to larger containers after a few weeks, and other plants will take two or three times as long. It pays to sit down with a calendar; select your in-container planting day; and then count back the number of days required to germinate that particular variety. The seed pack should provide you with information about days to germination.

It makes little sense to start vegetables that germinate and grow quickly—or that do not transplant well. They include beans, corn, and summer squash. Nor does it make sense to plant cool-weather crops, such as peas, radishes, and lettuce, indoors. They, too, are best sown directly into outdoor containers at the appropriate time.

The Right-Size Pot

Most vegetables will be happy in a 2-gallon container that's 12 inches in diameter and at least 12 inches deep. For larger vegetables, such as squash, a 4-gallon container is better. Shallow-rooted crops, such as lettuce, radishes, and herbs, need a container at least 6 inches in diameter with a 7-inch soil depth. For a mix of herbs in one container, allow 1 gallon of potting mix per plant. A 16-inch-diameter pot, for example, holds about 5½ gallons of mix, so it can support five plants. Use extra mix whenever possible.

Save your 4-gal. nursery containers and use them to grow vegetables. This single zucchini plant produced nine squashes.

Starting seed indoors is enormously satisfying. That 7-foot-tall tomato plant was once a tiny seed in your basement!

Tips for Growing from Seed

1 Sow a few seeds in each cell. A dampened pencil tip makes handling small seeds easier. Do not over-sow. It makes thinning more difficult.

2 Cover trays with plastic lids to raise the temperature of the tray. The warmer temperatures will improve germination. Remove the lids after germination.

3 When the seeds germinate, give them at least 12 hours of light. Seedlings that do not receive enough light will look leggy and pale.

4 Fertilize when plants develop a second set of leaves. Apply fertilizer at half the rate recommended by the manufacturer.

5 Use a fork to pry up and move plants to larger 4 x 4-in. pots when true leaves form. Select the healthiest looking seedlings for transplanting.

6 A couple of weeks before planting, "harden off" plants by bringing them outdoors during the day. Minimize exposure to direct sun during this period.

Parsley and chives live happily together in this terra-cotta pot. For more companion planting ideas, see below.

Companion Planting

Companion plants can assist in the growth of others by attracting beneficial insects and repelling harmful ones, and by providing nutrients, shade, and support. Rue, parsley, and geraniums, for example, help deter Japanese beetles. Marigolds discourage root-knot nematodes. Chives, onions, and garlic ward off aphids, spider mites, black spot, and powdery mildew. Some popular companions include

Basil with peppers or tomatoes
Chives with carrots or tomatoes
Nasturtiums with cabbage or cucumbers
Roses with garlic or onions
Strawberries with bush beans or lettuce
Parsley with asparagus or tomatoes
Beets with cabbage, onions, or lettuce

Some plants that do not enjoy sharing a container include

Carrots and dill
Cucumbers and potatoes or sage
Bush beans and onions, garlic, or chives
Mustard and beets
Tomatoes and potatoes

For additional examples of companion-planting combinations, go to www.companionplanting.net or to www.juliesedwick.com. Julie is a Master Gardener and one of the contributors to this book.

Exercise Caution

A startling number of plants, or parts thereof, are poisonous or toxic—more than 700 species in North America alone. If you have young children or pets with adventurous palates, avoid these plants altogether. Even if you don't, avoid combining any of these plants with container-grown edibles. For example, don't grow onions with daffodils, narcissus, or tulips. The flower bulbs will cause nausea, diarrhea, and vomiting if mistaken for onions. Parts of many plants grown for food are also toxic. Exercise caution when growing rhubarb, potatoes, and tomatoes on the patio—the leaves of all three are poisonous.

Other common garden plants that are highly toxic include the leaves and rootstock of irises, the buds of hydrangea, all parts of oleander, rhododendron, and azalea, all parts except the fruit of the sweet pea and everlasting pea (*Lathyrus* genus), the seeds of morning glory, pods and seeds from wisteria, berries from holly plants (*ilex* species), and most parts of the yew (*taxus* species). For a complete list, go to the U.S. Army Guide to Poisonous and Toxic Plants (http://chppm-www.apgea.army.mil/ento/PLANT.HTM). In addition to specifying which plant parts are dangerous, it lists symptoms should you ingest or, in some cases, touch the plants.

At least 3 percent of all poisonings are plant-related—including tomato leaves (above)—according to the National Safety Council.

Gardener's Tip

If the conditions are right, sow seeds directly into your
containers. If it's a bit too early in the season, turn your
container into a miniature cold frame by covering it with
plastic while the seeds are germinating.

"Recipes" for Edibles

The "recipes" on the following pages include container ideas and growing instructions for herbs and vegetables. I've mixed in some ornamentals here and there, too.

These "recipes," like those in the previous chapter, include plant names, preferred sun exposure, hardiness and heat zones, preferred potting mix, recommended pot sizes, and planting instructions. After each plant name, you'll find whether a plant is vegetable (V) or herb (H). Where I've included an ornamental, you'll see the same codes used in the previous chapter.

In general, "recipes" are arranged by when you can expect to harvest. Those at the beginning of the section are early producers, while those at the end of the section produce later in the season. Specific dates, of course, will vary by where you live. For a better idea of when you'll be able to harvest, note the plants' days to maturity.

Some of the recommended containers only include a single species. That's because it can be quite complex to deal with varying preferences of many of the plants. Also, it's often desirable to plant second crops. When the warm weather arrives, a pot of cilantro, for example, can be replanted with basil or culantro, a heat-loving herb that tastes like cilantro but has long, blade-like leaves. A pot of lettuce plants can give way to a lush crop of bush beans.

Full Sun to Partial Sun

Urn Your Salad

Spring is a time for celebration. Have some fun by mixing edibles with early ornamentals, as Kate Parisi did here.

- 4 lettuce *Lactuca sativa* mix of 'Salad Bowl' and 'Buttercrunch' (V) (NA, 12–1)
- 3 kale *Brassica oleracea* (V) (7–11, 6–1)
- 3 pansies *Viola* any pale blue cultivar (A) (9–1, NA)
- 3 grape hyacinth *Muscari aucheri* 'Blue Magic' (B) (6–9, 9–5)
- 3 golden creeping Jenny *Lysimachia nummularia* (P) (4–8, 8–1)
- Potting mix, light fertilization
- Pot or urn, 10-in. depth (min.)

Plant the grape hyacinth in the center of the pot or urn. Then surround it with kale and lettuce. Fill openings with pansies and creeping Jenny.

Full Sun to Partial Sun

A Little Lavender

I love containers that do more than sit there and look pretty. This creation combines the fragrance of lavender with an ever-changing mix of blossoms. Even the dusty miller changes its shade of green, depending on whether it's wet or dry.

- 2 lavender *Lavandula angustifolia* 'Blue Cushion' (H) (5–8, 8–5)
- 5 dusty miller *Senecio cineraria* 'Silver Dust' (P) (8–11, 12–1)
- 2 viola *Viola cornuta* (colors to suit) (P) (6–8, 8–6)
- Potting mix, light fertilization
- 14-in.-dia. terra-cotta pot, 10-in. depth (min.)

Plant the lavender in the center of the pot. Nestle the violas between them. Plant dusty miller around the perimeter. Exchange spent violas in summer for dwarf zinnias. Pinch dusty miller as needed.

Gardener's Tip

Unused seeds can be saved for several years. Store them in a closed container, such as a glass jar, in a cool, dry, and dark location. Or share the seeds with a friend!

Full Sun to Partial Sun

Spring Perk

Growing cilantro is easy. This clump was started from seed in mid-March under fluorescent lights. It was moved outdoors in mid-May.

- Cilantro seed *Coriandrum sativum* (H) (NA, 10–1)
- Potting mix, light fertilization
- 8-in.-dia. pot, 6-in. depth (min.)

To speed germination, crack seed husks, taking care not to damage the two seeds inside. Then follow the directions on pages 100–101. The cilantro should be ready to begin picking in 7–8 weeks. For a continuous harvest, it's a good idea to stagger sowing times. Once you move plants outdoors, place them where they'll get morning or late-afternoon sun but will be shaded during the hottest part of the day. When temperatures reach 75° F, cilantro will bolt. Then it's time to replant with a heat-loving herb, such as culantro.

Herb Medley 1

When combining herbs, don't crowd too many plants together, and don't mix fast growers with slowpokes. This trio gets along quite well.

- 1 pineapple mint *Mentha suaveolens* 'Variegata' (H) (6–9, 9–5)
- 2 oregano *Origanum majorana* or similar (H) (7–9, 10–2)
- 1 rosemary *Rosmarinus officinalis* (H) (8–11, 12–8)
- 2 lavender *Lavandula angustifolia* 'Fred Boutin' (H) (5–8, 8–5)
- Potting mix, light fertilization
- 18-in.-dia. pot, 12-in. depth (min.)

Set the rosemary in the center of your pot. Surround it with oregano, lavender, and pineapple mint. The mint will likely grow faster than the others, so turn the container so that the mint is to the north. Note: sage was also planted in this pot but couldn't compete. Next year, it will get its own pot.

Lettuce Bowl

For best ornamental effect, choose loose-leaf lettuce of differing colors. Harvest before the weather gets hot, or the leaves will taste bitter. Pot marigolds add color, and the petals add a spicy taste to salads.

- 6 lettuce *Lactuca sativa* mix of 'Salad Bowl' and 'Red Salad Bowl' or similar (V) (NA, 12–1)
- 2 pot marigold *Calendula officinalis* (A) (NA, 6–1)
- Potting mix, light fertilization
- 14-in. bowl, 7-in. depth (min.)

Plant seeds or seedlings into contai-ners in early spring, and space seeds 1 inch apart. Cover with ¼ inch of soil, and pat firm. When plants emerge, thin to 4–5 inches apart. Lettuce should be ready to pick in seven weeks. Fill open spaces with pot marigolds.

Testing Old Seeds

If you have old seeds, test them for viability before planting them. Lay three paper towels on a ceramic plate, and put 10 seeds on them. Cover the seeds with two paper towels, and dampen with a few tablespoons of water. Then slide the seeds and towels into a plastic bag, and put it somewhere warm (about 70° F). Check it every couple of days, and add more water if the towels begin to dry. After 7–10 days, count the seeds that have germinated. Multiply this number by 10 to get the germination percentage. If it is less than 70 percent, buy new seeds.

Herb Medley 2

Lobelia comes in several hues, but it's best known for its electric blues. I find it makes a pretty foil for my thyme collection.

- 3 lobelia *Lobelia erinus* 'Riviera Marine Blue' (P) (8–11, 8–1)
- Thyme *Thymus x citriodorus* 1 'Golden Lemon', 1 'Silver Queen', and 1 'Doone Valley' (H) (5–9, 9–6)
- Potting mix, light fertilization
- 5 x 14-in. trough, 6-in. depth (min.)

Plant lobelia in one row and the thyme in the other. When the former begins to look straggly in late summer, trim it, and wait until cooler temperatures revive it.

Full Sun

Endless Greens

Chard is one of those amazing plants that's difficult to eat fast enough. Not only is it mild tasting, but new leaves spring up a week or two after you cut it. For color, select 'Bright Lights' or 'Ruby Red' cultivars.

- 1 package of chard seeds *Beta vulgaris* (V) (6–10, 12–1)
- Potting mix, moderate fertilization
- Large tub or trough

Plant the seeds directly into your container in early spring, and cover with ½ inch of potting mix. Seeds germinate in 14–18 days. When the plants are 2 inches tall, thin to 4–5 inches apart in all directions. The plants can be harvested in about seven weeks. When picking, cut stems 1 inch above the level of the potting mix, and new leaves will grow.

Full Sun to Partial Sun

Berry Basket

Ever-bearing strawberries will provide fruit from early to late summer, taking a break only during hot weather. The plants, if protected by mulch, will produce for three years, at which point you should replace them. Some gardeners simply cut and plant the runners for a new batch of plants.

- 8 strawberry *Fragaria x ananassa* 'Quinault' (B) or similar ever-bearing hybrid (4–8, 8–1)
- Potting mix, moderate fertilization
- 12 x 24-in. wire trough with fiber liner, 8-in. depth (min.)

Plant seedlings so that the area where the leaves emerge (the crown) is even with—but not covered by—the potting mix surface. Space plants about 6 inches apart. Fertilize with a product high in phosphorus, such as one with a 1:2:1 ratio. Mulch with straw to within an inch of the crown. Cover with netting if birds begin to get to your berries before you do. Pick ripe berries regularly to prevent rot and the spread of disease.

Mess O' Carrots

Carrots are well suited to containers. They take up little space, and the potting mix allows them to grow straight without interference from compacted soil or stones. Other root crops, such as radishes, potatoes, and turnips, can be grown in a similar fashion.

- Carrot seeds *Daucus carota* 'Thumbelina' (V) (3–9, 10–1), 'Red-cored Chantenay' (V) (4–9, 10–1), or other compact cultivar
- Potting mix, moderate fertilization
- Box container 12 x 24 in., twice the root length deep (12 in. min.)

For an early crop, sow seeds indoors in late winter or early spring. Sow directly in the container in which you expect them to mature. Carrots do not transplant well and are fast growers. Move planted containers outdoors in April. Or sow seeds outdoors in containers in April. In either case, space seeds 1 inch apart. Thin to 3 inches apart in all directions. Begin pulling carrots five to seven weeks later.

Double Your Crop in a Raised Bed

Raised beds are a variation of container gardening for gardeners who don't want to sever their ties to the earth. Filled with garden soil and compost, the enclosures may be thought of as containers without bottoms.

- Lettuce, any variety
- Spinach, any variety
- Tomatoes, any variety
- Loam, compost, moderate fertilization
- Raised bed container

Plant your lettuce and spinach early, and poke in tomato plants when the weather has warmed. By the time you've harvested the greens seven to eight weeks later, the tomatoes will have filled out the vacated space. Raised beds can be purchased premade or built from scratch. A good size is 10 inches deep by 3 feet wide by 6 feet long.

Growing edibles is more about good pickings than looking pretty, but that doesn't mean they have to be eyesores.

Full Sun

Cherry Tomato Bonanza

There's nothing better than ripe and sun-warmed cherry tomatoes fresh off the vine. The Husky series cultivars I grow supply more than 150 fruits per plant in August and September on vines that grow to 4 feet tall. Other dwarf cherry cultivars, such as 'Tumbling Tom Red', have shorter habits. Choose vines that are resistant to verticillium wilt and fusarium wilt (often signified as VF).

- **2 dwarf cherry tomato *Lycopersicon esculentum* 'Husky Cherry Red VF' Husky series (V) (11–15, 12–1)**
- **Potting mix, high fertilization**
- **24 x 24-in. box, 20-in. depth (min.)**

Start plants indoors in early spring. Transplant to 4 x 4-inch pots after four weeks. Begin to harden off plants in mid to late spring. Then transplant to large outdoor containers in late spring. For every 4-square-foot area, grow two plants about 18 inches apart. Bury several inches of the stems as well as the roots. Pick fruits about 70 days later. This hybrid requires staking.

Full Sun to Partial Sun

Gift Basket

Have a friend with no space to plant a vegetable garden? Put together a mixed basket of veggies. This one includes Swiss chard, lettuce, a variegated nasturtium, and pole beans that turn from purple to green when cooked.

- **4 purple pod pole bean seeds (V) (zones NA)**
- **3 Swiss chard *Beta vulgaris* (V) (6–10, 12–1)**
- **3 lettuce plants *Lactuca sativa* 'Black Seeded Simpson' or similar (V) (NA, 12–1)**
- **1 nasturtium *Tropaeolum majus* Alaska series (P) (10–11, 12–1)**
- **Potting mix, light fertilization**
- **12-in.-dia. bushel basket, 10-in. depth (min.)**

Insert a U-shaped bamboo stake for the beans. Then plant the seeds in early to mid spring. Place three bean seeds around the base of each stake. Thin to one each when the plants are 4–5 inches tall. They will grow quickly, and beans will be ready for picking in about 70 days. Plant the other seeds around the basket perimeter, spacing them 1 inch apart. Thin to suit once they are 2–3 inches tall. You may substitute snap peas for the beans.

Gardener's Tip

Remove female zucchini blossoms (the ones attached to the fruits) to prevent rot from forming. Harvest male blossoms regularly, and refrigerate them until you have enough for frying or mixing into your scrambled eggs.

Full Sun

Purple and White

This combination of purple and white eggplants in a large, self-watering container thrived throughout the summer months, producing almost a dozen 10-inch-long fruits. First picked was this white eggplant, shown here in mid-August.

- Eggplant *Solanum melongena* 'Black Beauty' (V) (10–12, 12–1)
- Eggplant *Solanum melongena* 'Cloud Nine' (V) (10–12, 12–1)
- Potting mix, moderate fertilization
- 12 x 30-in. trough, 12-in. depth (min.)

Plant eggplant seeds in late winter or early spring, or buy plants in late spring. Move outdoors in large containers only after warm weather arrives and all danger of frost has passed. Fruits are typically ready for harvesting 70 days after transplanting and 100–150 days after sowing.

Full Sun

Zukes Galore

Zucchini plants have huge, gorgeous leaves and big, edible yellow flowers; and they produce more fruit than you'll be able to use. On the flip side, they take up a lot of space (a 4 x 4-foot area is typical), so you may need to move them off the deck or patio as they mature. Novel, compact cultivars, such as 'Eight Ball' (small, sphere-shaped fruits) and the hybrid 'Raven' (3 x 3-foot area; 7- to 8-inch-long, 2-inch-diameter fruits) are suitable for container gardening. You may also grow other types of squash, such as the colorful acorn squash cultivar 'Festival' or the tiny pumpkin 'Bumpkin', but the vines of either require trellising.

■ Zucchini *Cucurbita pepo* 'Spineless Beauty' hybrid
■ Potting mix with 10% sand, moderate fertilization
■ 12 x 30-in. trough, 12-in. depth (min.)

Plant seeds in late spring or early summer directly into your outdoor container. Sow three seeds for each desired plant, and thin to one once they have grown to 3 inches tall. Allow at least 2 square feet per plant. Plants will grow very quickly and bear fruit within seven to eight weeks of sowing.

Full Sun to Partial Sun

Winter Beauty

Ornamental kale is a favorite for long-lasting, colorful containers once the weather starts to cool. Available in colors ranging from white (shown) to pink, purple, and red, it's planted here with lavender pansies by designer Ruth Zelig. Kale also works well with other frost-hardy ornamentals, such as sedums and asters.

■ Ornamental kale *Brassica oleracea* 'Chidori White' (V) (7–11, 6–1)
■ Pansies, any variety (fall colors)
■ Decorative elements, such as pumpkin, colored corn, and gourds
■ Potting mix, moderate fertilization
■ 12-in.-dia. urn, 10-in. depth (min.)

Sow seeds 6–10 weeks before the average first frost date, and place pots in a cool basement. The seeds need light to germinate; so place them near a window; and do not cover them with mix. Move plants outside when the cool weather arrives, and transplant to a decorative urn. The colors start to show with cold weather and frost. Kale survives to temperatures well below freezing and lasts into the winter in many zones.

Chapter 6

Shrubs, Trees, and Fruits

A large container planting of a tree, shrub, or fruit is a long-term commitment. I once owned a large potted gardenia that faithfully bloomed for more than a dozen years before succumbing to an unexpected frost. Several of my gardening friends have nurtured citrus trees planted in containers for longer than that. Larger doesn't necessarily mean more care. In fact, trees and shrubs often require less labor than smaller annual plantings.

hey don't need to be planted every year, and they require less fertilizer and less-frequent watering. They may, however, need to be repotted every three or four years. And some may need to be moved inside, depending on the species' hardiness and the lowest winter temperatures where you live.

Trees and shrubs are sold in three ways: bare root, balled and bagged in burlap, and container grown. For my container garden, I prefer the last. There is greater variety of species from which to choose, and you get all of the roots—not just those that survived digging up the tree. If possible, pull the plant from its container and examine its roots. They should be a healthy white or off-white color—not black, slimy, or smelly. Check to be sure container-

grown trees are not root bound (have a dense mass). There should be few, if any, roots emerging from the container's drain holes. If you simply can't resist the mark-down on a root-bound plant, be sure to cut away some of the roots before replanting it in a new container. Score them with a utility knife from top to bottom at 4-inch intervals. Tear away the severed roots, and loosen the remaining root mass with your hands prior to planting.

When buying a tree, examine its form, too. I once bought a dogwood at a deep discount. It had fewer branches on one side than the other, but I thought it would fill out in a season or two. I've since learned that my dogwood was probably grown under crowded conditions. The misshapen form has taken many years to improve. Look for symmetrical specimens with good foliage and color. Avoid trees with branch tips that are dead or dying, root balls that are broken or loosely connected to the trunk, and damaged bark or branches.

Buying shrubs is similar to buying trees. In addition to the advice previously mentioned, look for compact specimens, and avoid the ones with sparse branches. A compact, well-branched shrub means that it has received adequate sunlight and will be more likely to thrive. Avoid plants with dull-colored leaves and small, tight buds that seem dry.

If the location where a tree or shrub was grown is not on the label, ask your supplier about its origin. Plants grown in the region where you live will probably do better than plants that will require a season to adapt to a new climate. Be sure that the tree or shrub you buy will be able to withstand the temperature lows in your area. Note: for standards (shrubs trained to take the form of trees), select species that are hardy to two zones colder than your own.

Designing with Shrubs

As discussed in Chapter 1, landscaping with containers is the most challenging—and rewarding—aspect of container gardening. Shrubs in containers offer sheer mass that few other container plants can match. Species with dense habits serve beautifully as foils to flowering containers placed in front of them. They can also be used as barriers, as borders, and as privacy screens.

Shrub habits range from conical and columnar to rounded and arching. (See below.) Choose the shape that best suits your situation. Columnar species, for example, suit the simple geometry of contemporary homes. Arching shrubs may be better suited to Victorian house styles. Small mounding shrubs are good for accents and barriers.

Shrubs can also take center stage as a focal point. They often have spectacular displays of flowers, and many produce colorful fruits and berries.

Trees generally have single trunks, while shrubs have several small trunks growing from a common base. Some shrubs look like trees; others stay close to the ground. The illustrations show some of the common shrub forms, or habits.

Prostrate

Columnar

Arching

Conical

Mounding

When shrubs are trained to take the form of trees, they're called "standards." The lower branches are removed, leaving a "trunk." Good shrubs for turning into standards include boxwoods, hibiscuses, roses, hydrangeas, and lilacs.

Seek out dwarf or miniature tree and shrub hybrids for container plantings. New butterfly bush cultivars, for example, grow no more than a few feet tall and 2 feet wide, bloom continuously, and don't need deadheading.

Gardener's Tip

A simple way to tell whether a tree or shrub was properly maintained at the garden center is to check the height of the potting soil. It should reach within an inch of the container rim and feel moist to the touch.

Designing with Trees

Most trees can be grown in containers, at least for a while. Trees that grow to more than 20 feet tall are best left in the ground. Shorter trees, however, can thrive in containers for many years. (See "Trees for Containers" on page 123.)

Trees, like shrubs, can be used as foils, barriers, privacy screens, and focal points. Most potted trees create a strong vertical element, perfect for creating a balance with horizontal elements, such as fences, walls, and structures that are more horizontal than vertical.

Container-planted trees sometimes look better with plantings around the base of the tree. I prefer ground covers, such as myrtle, creeping Jenny (*Lysimachia nummularia*), and moss, which are shallow-rooted and won't compete too much with the tree for water and nutrients.

Many shrubs and trees can overwinter in their containers with a bit of help. (See page 149.) Just be sure your container is freeze proof and that your plant can survive outdoor temperatures in your zone. (See the plant hardiness and heat zone maps on pages 150–151.) Note: trees growing in containers are more susceptible to damage from the cold than those grown in the ground, so it's wise to select species hardy to two zones colder than your own if you plan to leave the trees outside during winter. Insulating the roots by wrapping the container with insulation and burlap is also recommended. (See page 149.)

Container Sizes

When selecting a container for a shrub or tree, choose one that's a few inches larger than the plant's root mass. A plant that has filled out its 12-inch-diameter nursery container, for example, can be planted in a 15- to 18-inch decorative container. The larger the container, the greater its chance of survival, the fewer waterings it will need, and the longer it will be before you'll have to repot it.

Trees exhibit a multitude of growing habits, only some of which are illustrated here. Other habits include oval, pyramidal, and clump, or multi-trunked. In addition to overall shape, consider bark texture, blossoms, branch shapes (of deciduous trees), winter foliage (of evergreens), and whether the tree will produce fruits, nuts, or berries.

Conical

Columnar

Open

Closed (rounded)

Weeping

Tree and Shrub Planting Basics

1 Select a container with at least 3 inches of room for root growth around the sides. Then measure the root-ball depth.

2 Measure the pot depth, and subtract the root-ball depth. Subtract 2 inches from the remainder, and fill with mix to this depth.

3 Choose a potting mix with sandy loam soil, compost, and peat moss. Mix in a slow-release fertilizer, and add moisture-holding gel crystals.

4 Place plant in the center of the pot, and fill around it to a height that's level with the root ball top.

5 Add some mulch to slow evaporation.

6 Water thoroughly, and place in filtered light until the plant is established.

"Recipes" for Trees and Shrubs

The following "recipes" include container ideas and growing instructions for trees and shrubs. They include plant names, preferred sun exposure, hardiness and heat zones, preferred potting mix, recommended pot sizes, and planting instructions. After each plant name, you'll find whether the plant is a tree (T), shrub (S), or woody vine (V). Where I've included ornamentals, you'll see the same codes used in chapter 4. "Recipes" are presented in no particular order.

The plant hardiness map on page 151 will assist you in deciding whether you can leave your containers outdoors during the winter. The plant's hardiness zone is an indication of whether it will survive the average minimum winter temperatures in your area. Keep in mind, however, that the hardiness recommendations are for plants that are grown in the ground. Container-planted trees and shrubs may have to tolerate much colder temperatures if the containers are exposed to the weather. When choosing a tree or shrub for a container, it's often wise to select species that are hardy to colder zones than your own. For example, if you live in zone 6, chose a tree that is hardy to zone 4. The heat-zone map on page 150 will give you an idea of whether a tree species can tolerate hot weather.

Partial Sun to Shade

Endless Color

Hydrangeas, in their many varieties, are prolific flowering shrubs. Their large, showy blossoms can change from green to white to pink or blue to mauve to cream during the course of a summer. This cultivar blooms continually from early summer until early fall.

- *Hydrangea macrophylla* 'Bailmer' Endless Summer series (S) (6–8, 9–6)
- Potting mix, light fertilization
- 12-in.-dia. pot, 10-in. depth (min.)

Mix low-nitrogen and high-phosphate fertilizer in potting mix prior to planting. Add aluminum sulfate (acidifier) for blue blossoms and dolomitic lime for pink blossoms. Mulch after planting. Use your potted hydrangea as a portable color accent in the garden. The container in the photo spent early summer in a bed of azaleas and blue bells. Come September, when other blooms were fading, its blossoms continued to brighten our deck.

Full Sun to Partial Sun

Boxwoods for Good Behavior

Boxwoods make wonderful accents on the patio. Choose one that's a slow grower, such as this one, and you will be rewarded with a well-behaved, low-maintenance shrub. Not fussy, it tolerates some shade as well.

- Boxwood *Buxus microphylla* 'Winter Gem' (S) or similar (4–9, 11–6)
- Potting mix, light fertilization
- 16 x 16-in. planter box, 14-in. depth (min.)

Mix slow-release, balanced fertilizer in potting mix, and plant the boxwood according to the instructions on page 119. Trim as needed.

Gardener's Tip

Poor drainage in large containers can cause early mortality of your trees or shrubs. Be sure that your container has at least two ¾-inch drainage holes for every square foot of container base.

Full Sun to Partial Sun

Flower Guard

Hibiscus is a tireless bloomer throughout the warm-weather months. Use in standard form near an entry, or stand one in the middle of a group of containers to add height and color.

- **Hibiscus rosa-sinensis (S) (10–5, 12–1)**
- **Bark mulch**
- **Potting mix, moderate fertilization**
- **12-in.-dia. pot, 10-in. depth (min.)**

Mix slow-release, balanced fertilizer in potting mix, and plant the hibiscus in the center of the pot, according to the instructions on page 119. Spread mulch around the base, but keep it an inch or two away from the trunk. You must bring hibiscus inside if there is any chance of freezing weather. Prune branches in the spring to maintain shape and to promote new growth.

Full Sun

Citrus Circus

Lemon trees are evergreen and fragrant, often blossom for several months, and produce lots of delicious fruit for winter and early spring. This popular hybrid grows 6–12 feet but can be kept in check with pruning.

- **Lemon tree *Citrus x meyeri* 'Meyer Improved' (T) (9–11, 12–1)**
- **Potting mix**
- **22-in. pot, 30-in. depth (min.)**
- **10-in. stakes**

Mix 10 percent sand, 10 percent loam, and slow-release fertilizer that's high in nitrogen with potting mix, such as a citrus-palm fertilizer. Plant the tree according to the instructions on page 119. Apply a supplementary fertilizer in spring and early summer using a water-soluble product. Thin fruit clusters to a single fruit when lemons are the size of golf balls. In cold climates, bring citrus trees inside.

Full Sun to Partial Sun

Sicilian Dreaming

Can't afford a trip to the Mediterranean at the moment? Plant a fast-growing fig tree in a pot, and enjoy its highly ornamental foliage and delicious fruit from home.

- **Fig *Ficus carica* 'Blanche' (S) (6–10, 9–6)**
- **Potting mix, light fertilization**
- **20-in.-dia. pot, 18-in. depth (min.)**

Mix 10 percent sand, 20 percent loam, and slow-release, balanced fertilizer with potting mix. Plant as shown on page 119. Avoid fertilizers with high nitrogen content, or most of the growth will go to foliage, not the fruit.

Trees for Containers

Most trees can be grown in containers. In fact, that's typically how you will find them at the nursery. Large species or fast-growing trees, however, will quickly outgrow even your largest container. To save yourself pruning and repotting chores, choose slow-growing and dwarf trees for your containers. Here are some species that are suitable:

Arborvitae (*Thuja*)
Avocado (*Persea americana*)
Bottlebrush (*Callistemon rigidus*)
Carolina silverbell (*Halesia carolina*)
Chinese dogwood (*Cornus kousa*)
Colonnade apple (*Malus*)
Crabapple (*Malus*)
Crape myrtle (*Lagerstroemia indica*)
Fig (*Ficus carica*)
Hinoki false cypress (*Chamaecyparis obtusa*)
Japanese maple (*Acer palmatum*)
Juniper (*Juniperus*)
River birch (*Betula nigra*)
Sourwood (*Oxydendrum arboreum*)
Star magnolia (*Magnolia stellata*)
White fringe tree (*Chionanthus virginicus*)
Yew (*Taxus*)

Full Sun to Partial Sun

Patio Orchard

Many cultivars of apple trees can be successfully grown on a patio or deck in large pots. Grown on dwarf root stocks, tree height is limited to 9–10 feet. To ensure pollination of fruit trees that do not self-pollinate, group in twos or threes. Check with your supplier for recommended pollination partners.

- Dwarf apple *Malus domestica* 'Pixie' (T) or similar (5–8, 9–1)
- Potting mix, sand, and loam; moderate fertilization
- 24-in.-dia. pot, 30-in. depth (min.)

Mix 20 percent sand, 20 percent loam, two cups of lime, and slow-release fertilizer with potting mix. Plant the tree as described on page 119. Supplement fertilizer in spring and summer with a water-soluble fertilizer. Use stakes to provide support. Insulate pots in areas where freezing occurs.

Full Sun to Partial Sun

Show Me Your Palm

Palms come in many varieties and are great in containers. This cycad looks like a palm but isn't. Nevertheless, this slow-grower strikes a very believable tropical pose.

- **1 sago palm *Cycas revoluta* (T) (8–15, 12–6)**
- **Rounded stones (as mulch)**
- **Potting mix, light fertilization**
- **20 x 20-in. planter, 15-in. depth (min.)**

Mix about 20 percent sand and palm fertilizer with your potting mix. Plant and mulch with stones. Bring the plant inside for winter (unless you live in the tropics), and give it as much light as possible to ensure survival.

Full Sun to Partial Sun

Lacy Evergreen

The western arborvitae has an airy, light presence compared with other species and is well-suited as a focal point in an informal garden bed. Change out the under-plantings yearly. This drought-resistant arrangement from Proven Winners combines the frilly pink blossoms of the cuphea with a compact silvery helichrysum culti-var and a plectranthus that puts forth spires of sky-blue flowers.

- **3 cuphea *Cuphea ilavea* 'Flamenco Tango' Flamenco series (P) (10–15, 12–6)**
- **3 licorice plants *Helichrysum petiolare* (P) 'Petite Licorice' (9–11, 12–1)**
- **3 spurflowers *Plectranthus amboinicus* 'Blue Yonder' (P) (9–11, 12–1)**
- **Western arborvitae *Thuja plicata* (T) (6–8, 8–6)**
- **Potting mix, light fertilization**
- **30-in.-dia. ceramic or terra-cotta pot**

Mix slow-release fertilizer and 20 percent sand with potting mix, and plant the arborvitae in the center of the pot. Alternately plant the cuphea, licorice plant, and plectranthus around the tree. Supplement with water-soluble fertilizer in spring and summer.

Partial Sun to Shade

Take the Silk Road

Looking for an exotic tree? The silk tree, with its powder-puff blossoms, fragrance, and leaves that fold when touched, is intriguing. Note: in warm climates, these trees are often invasive. Chose a cultivar that does not produce seed!

- 1 mimosa silk tree *Albizia* 'Summer Chocolate' (T) (6–10, NA)
- 3 *Torenia* 'Gilded Grape' Catalina series (P) (10–11, 12–3)
- 3 *Tradescantia* 'Concord Grape' (5–9, 9–5)
- 2 *Setcreasea pallida* 'Purple Heart' (P) (7–12, 12–1)
- 4 coleus *Solenostemon scutellariodes* 'Dipt in Wine' (P) (10–12, 12–1)
- 3 *Hebe* 'Purple Shamrock' (S) (8–9, NA)
- Potting soil, moderate fertilization
- 14-in. x 26-in.pot, 27-in. depth

Mix slow-release fertilizer with potting soil. Plant the mimosa at the back of the container, and plant the coleus in the middle. Then plant the tradescantia (tall flowers) to either side of the coleus. Alternately plant the torenia (orange flowers), secreasea (purple leaves), and hebe (far right, not in bloom).

Full Sun to Partial Sun

Inspired Spiral

This dwarf species of boxwood is quite dense and slow growing, making it ideal for topiary.

- Boxwood *Buxus sempervirens* 'Suffruticosa' (S) (6–8, 9–3)
- 3 lobelia *Lobelia erinus* 'Riviera Marine Blue' (P) (8–11, 8–1)
- 3 scented geraniums *Pelargonium* 'Concolor Lace' (P) (9–11, 12–1)
- Potting mix, light fertilization
- 14-in.-dia. urn, 14-in. depth (min.)

Plant the boxwood at the back of the urn as described on page 119. In front of it, alternately plant the scented geranium and lobelia. Maintain topiary shape with regular trimming.

High Climbers

Roses have been cultivated for thousands of years. They can be successfully grown in containers. This one has full double white flowers that begin blooming in late spring. If you prefer red, choose the 'Blaze' cultivar.

- **2 roses** *Rosa* **'Iceberg' (climbing variety) (S) or any climbing species (5–9, 9–5)**
- **Sturdy trellis**
- **Potting mix, light fertilization**
- **20-in. dia. pot, 20-in. depth (min.)**

Mix high-phosphate, slow-release fertilizer in the potting mix, and plant as shown on page 119. Frequently supplement with light doses of water-soluble fertilizer. Roses are susceptible to fungal infections, so place containers where there is good air circulation and lots of sun. Prune to maintain air circulation as needed. Weave runners into the trellis, or use wire to secure runners along the path you'd like them to take.

South of the Border

Native to Central and South America, mandevilla has become a popular vine for container planting in the North. This cultivar sports deep red blossoms for the entire summer. Other cultivars are white or pink and sometimes fragrant. Mandevilla can be grown as a vertical focal point or over a trellis for privacy.

- **1 mandevilla** *Mandevilla* **'Sunmanderemi' Sun Parasol series (V) or similar (10–15, 12–1)**
- **Stakes, trellis, or twine hung from eave**
- **Potting mix, light fertilization**
- **12-in.-dia. pot, 10-in. depth (min.)**

Mix slow-release fertilizer in potting mix, and plant according to the instructions on page 119. Apply mulch. Supplement fertilizer during spring and summer with a water-soluble product. In most climates, mandevilla must be brought inside during the winter. I cut mine back to 2 feet tall, put it near a basement window, and water once every two or three weeks.

Full Sun to Partial Sun

Make an Impression

Wisteria's long clusters of flowers are beautiful and fragrant in spring. Unfortunately, this fast-growing woody vine is difficult to manage in the garden. Its roots are invasive and it needs constant pruning. Containers are a good solution for this unruly plant.

- 1 wisteria *Wisteria floribunda* (V) (5–9, 9–3)
- Potting mix, sand, loam; light fertilization
- 14-in.-dia. pot, 12-in. depth (min.)

Choose a shoot or young plant, and stake upright. Remove the side shoots. Prune top shoots as needed to maintain a tree-like canopy. When the stem is strong enough, remove the stake. Avoid the use of fertilizers with high ratios of nitrogen to encourage blossoms.

Shrubs and trees, unlike other container plantings, will be with you for many years. Choose a species that you love.

Partial Sun to Shade

Serene Maple

There are many Japanese maple cultivars and varieties, and most of them can be grown in containers. Colors range from pale green to peach to deep red and are sometimes variegated. Autumn color displays are often spectacular. Leaf shapes range from the familiar five-point pattern to lacy finger shapes. In winter, branch structure can be intriguing. This specimen, grown by Bob La Pointe, includes a mix of yellows, greens, and reds.

- **Japanese maple *Acer palmatum* 'Kiyohime' (T) (6–8, 8–2) or any dwarf or semi-dwarf cultivar**
- **Potting mix, light fertilization**
- **15-in.-dia. pot, 20-in. depth (min.)**

Mix a slow-release fertilizer with potting mix, 30 percent loam, and 30 percent sand. Plant as described on page 119. Supplement with a water-soluble fertilizer during spring and early summer only. In cold climates, insulate containers or bring plants into a shed or basement for the winter.

Full Sun to Partial Sun

Holly Hobby

I love to have holly on hand for winter floral arrangements and decorations, but I don't have enough space in my yard for a large shrub. A slow-growing dwarf holly planted in a container is the perfect solution.

- **Holly *Ilex x meserveae* 'Blue Baron' (S) (5–9, 9–5)**
- **Potting mix, sand, loam; light fertilization**
- **12-in.-dia. pot, 10-in. depth (min)**

Mix slow-release fertilizer in potting mix and acidifier (sulfur) according to the manufacturer's directions. Plant the holly shrub according to the instructions on page 119. Apply mulch, such as bark chips. Supplement fertilizer during the spring and summer with a water-soluble product. If you want berries, pair this hybrid with any of the blue holly female cultivars, such as 'Blue Princess'. Holly bushes are hardy to temperatures well below freezing, but you should shelter them from the wind, and insulate the container in cold climates. (See page 149.)

Ongoing Maintenance

The best thing about container gardens is that they are so manageable. Digging is minimal, weeds are few, and pests and diseases are easier to detect and deter. Pinching, pruning, and harvesting are easier, too, because the plants are close at hand. Some chores, however, require extra attention. Container gardens are more susceptible to damage from the sun on a hot day than are gardens planted in the ground.

ou may also have to fertilize plants in containers more frequently. They have a relatively small area from which to draw nutrients, which all that watering can drain away quickly. And because container gardening allows you to grow plants that would not otherwise survive in your climate, you may have the added chore of bringing plants indoors in the fall.

Too much shade can be a maintenance issue, too. Container gardens are often placed near the house or some other structure that blocks the sun for part of the day. In addition, lighting conditions change with the season. In late June in North America, for example, the sun is at its highest point in the sky, and solar radiation is at its most intense. As the sun's path becomes lower, plants that were once in full sun may be in shade. You may need to move your pots later in the summer to improve their exposure to the sun. You can also increase available light by using reflective materials around plants. A white wall or fence reflects a large amount of solar radiation.

Many vegetables and flowers require a minimum of six hours of sunlight every day to thrive. Check light requirements for specific plants before you make your purchases to be sure you can accommodate their needs. Similarly, you will have to ensure that plants aren't getting too much sun and that they do not become stressed by too much heat. Average daily temperatures peak in July and August. If possible, move containers of heat-sensitive plants to cooler locations.

Watering Your Containers

The potting mix in a 10-inch-diameter pot that stands 10 inches tall holds about 2 quarts of water. Through evaporation and transpiration, that water can disappear quickly on a hot day. Unlike the roots of earth-grown plants, containerized roots have nowhere to go for more water. As the container dries, it begins to bake—and so do the plants.

To avoid dried-out plants, check your containers at least once a day. Wilting plants, of course, are a sure sign that they need water. You can also feel the mix a couple of inches below the surface to determine whether it's moist. (Checking only the surface will not tell you.) On very hot or windy days, check your containers twice.

Most of us don't need to be told how to water plants, but it's good to review the basics because both overwatering and underwatering can cause problems. In general, apply water until you see it running from the drain holes. Be observant though. If the potting soil has been allowed to become very dry and has pulled away from the container, water may run down the inner surface of the pot and out the drain holes instead of being absorbed by the mix. In such cases, place the container, if possible, into a basin filled with a few inches of water. The potting mix will rehydrate in an hour or so. Submersion watering works great for baskets, too. If a container, such as a wooden box or barrel, is too big to submerge, lay the end of your hose on the mix surface, and turn on the hose so that there is a slow trickle. Leave it that way for an hour.

Watering Aids

Watering cans are necessities, but you can save tiresome trips to the spigot by buying an extra hose that you can dedicate to your container garden. By installing a diverter on your spigot, you can use one hose for regular chores and the other for watering. Look for a nozzle that allows for multiple spray patterns. Mine has forceful "cone" and "jet" settings as well as "shower" and "soaker" settings, which are the ones I find

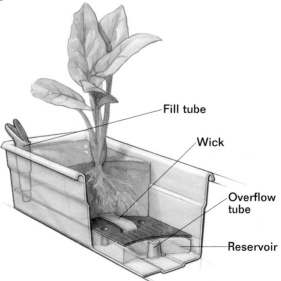

Self-watering containers (right) moisten soil in several ways. Most units rely on evaporation from the reservoir and on capillary action via a wick. Some also have channels that allow the soil to be in contact with the water.

Fill tube

Wick

Overflow tube

Reservoir

A self-watering container (left) has a reservoir in its base.

Absorbent gel crystals (above) extend time between waterings. Make several holes in the soil, and fill halfway with crystals.

Moisture-holding pads (below) help prevent dry-out and are well suited to hanging baskets and window boxes.

Gardener's Tip

If you are having trouble keeping your planted containers moist during the hottest part of the summer, try grouping them together. The foliage will create a canopy to shade the mix, keep it cool, and slow evaporation. Grouped containers will make watering chores easier, too.

useful for watering my containers. Buy a wand nozzle, too, if you have multiple baskets that will need watering. The wand allows you to reach overhead easily, and the low-pressure setting does not disturb potting mixes or plants.

You can often cut watering chores by half, or more, with the use of self-watering containers. Fill them, and check the reservoir level every few days. Virtually all types of planters, from pots to window boxes, are now available with self-watering features. Typically, they include a watering tube that extends through the potting mix to a reservoir below. Reservoir sizes vary, but capacities of several gallons are typical. Retrofit kits allow you to add a self-watering capability to many sizes of containers at low cost.

Two cautions about self-watering containers: in rainy weather they may work too well, keeping the potting mix too moist for many plants; and small self-watering containers are not good for growing large plants, such as tomatoes, eggplant, and squash. For that, you'll need containers that are at least 11 inches tall.

Other aids include gel crystals and water-absorbing mats. Gel crystals must be added to potting mix prior to planting. They absorb up to 200 times their weight in water, keeping the soil moist longer. Take care not to use too many crystals; a teaspoon for an 8-inch-diameter pot is enough. Buy crystals made with potassium-based polymers, not salts, which can harm plants. When the crystals break down after several years, they'll work as a fertilizer.

Water-absorbing mats also absorb and hold water. They're well suited for use in hanging baskets that dry out quickly. Simply cut the mat to fit the inside of the basket liner. Fill the container with potting mix, and water it until the mat is fully hydrated (when water begins to leak through the basket).

Drip Irrigation

Drip-irrigation systems, the ultimate solution to simplifying watering chores, work as well with container plantings as they do with earth gardens. Drip irrigation delivers small amounts of water directly to the base of the plant. With some systems, the gallons-per-hour (gph) flow of the drippers is adjustable; with others you must install the dripper that is best suited to the container size it's going to irrigate. For example, a small pot may only need a ½-gph dripper, but a larger one may require a 1-gph dripper. A tree in a large container may require a 2-gph dripper. Another benefit to drip irrigation is that it can be automated with a timer. Should you go away for vacation, it will water your containers for you.

Begin any drip-irrigation system installation by checking the number of gallons your water source can deliver in an hour. With the spigot fully open, determine how much water is delivered in a minute. Then multiply by 60 to get the number of gallons it can deliver in an hour. This information will be useful when determining how many

Reduce Water Usage

The first rule of water conservation is to use only what your plants need and no more. Most annuals and herbs, for example, thrive with a watering schedule that allows the potting mix to nearly dry out. Fast-growing leafy plants, on the other hand, may need more frequent watering and consistently moist soil. There are other ways to save water, too:

- Choose drought-tolerant plants.
- Mulch to slow evaporation and reduce the number of times you'll need to water containers. Mulches can be natural, such as bark or bark chips, or man-made, including plastic sheeting and landscape fabric. I prefer the look of a finely textured mulch, such as buckwheat hulls, for containers.
- Utilize windbreaks to slow evaporation. Determine the direction of the prevailing wind in your yard, and position containers so they'll be sheltered from it, whether that's by a fence, hedge, large stone, or structure.
- Water the potting mix, not the foliage. This ensures that water gets to the roots instead of evaporating from the leaves.
- Enhance potting mix with organic materials that absorb water. You can also add water-holding polymers to your mix.
- Consider installing a drip-irrigation system. It can be adjusted to deliver precisely the amount of water your plants need, with very little waste.
- Collect rain water in a rain barrel, and use it to water your plants. Today's rain barrels are stylish, lightweight, and come equipped with handy features, including insect screens and spigots.

Installing Patio Drip Irrigation

1 Assemble the adapter, and attach it to a spigot that has an anti-siphon valve and pressure regulator.

2 Insert the tubing into an adaptor, and run the line to the first planter. Use clamps to secure the tubing to the posts, soffits, and the underside of railings.

3 Use a tee to make branches, such as to a hanging basket. The barbed fitting ends make assembly easy; no glue is required. Cut the tubing with scissors.

4 Install the dripper at the branch end.

5 Bend the tubing, and insert it into the clamp at the end of the run to stop any further flow of water.

6 This dripper flows at a rate of about ½ gph.

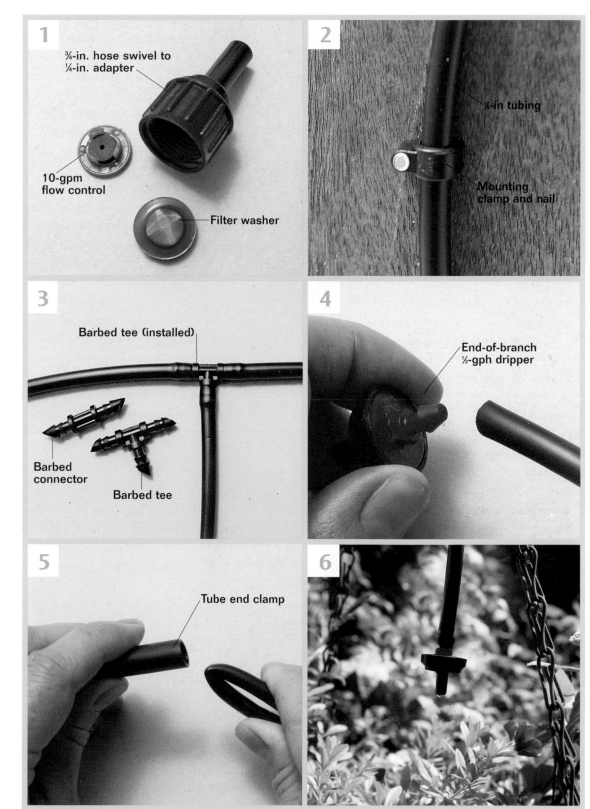

1 — ¾-in. hose swivel to ¼-in. adapter — 10-gpm flow control — Filter washer

2 — ¼-in tubing — Mounting clamp and nail

3 — Barbed tee (installed) — Barbed connector — Barbed tee

4 — End-of-branch ½-gph dripper

5 — Tube end clamp

6

Rain barrels have had a cosmetic makeover in recent years. This rainwater urn sits under the downspout, is made of rugged polypropylene, and comes with a spigot and an insect screen.

emitters your system can handle. For most container gardens, you will have more than enough capacity.

Drip-irrigation kits are an inexpensive way to get started, but they often don't include important components, such as pressure regulators and anti-siphon valves. A better approach is to draw a plan for your system, and then buy the components you'll need.

Container Fertilization

Many brands of potting mix today already contain small amounts of fertilizer mixed in at the factory. Others don't. Regardless, it's wise to add a slow-release granular synthetic fertilizer or organic fertilizer to the mix before you plant. That way, nutrients will become available to plants gradually, throughout the growing season. Fill your container about halfway, stir in the fertilizer, and then add more potting mix and plants. During the growing season, you can supplement these nutrients with liquid fertilizers that can be applied while you water.

How much fertilizer to add is a difficult question. It will depend upon plant type, container size, time of season, the amount of rain that falls upon your containers, and the type and grade of fertilizer you use. I have found that it's best to apply fertilizer at about half the manufac-

turer's recommendation when planting. I then apply light doses of liquid fertilizer every two weeks during the spring and early summer. During late summer, I reduce applications to once every three weeks.

Keep in mind that fast-growing and long-blooming annuals need more fertilizer than bulbs, perennials, herbs, shrubs, and trees. With vegetables that bear fruit, such as tomatos, peppers, and eggplants, heavier applications may be necessary.

Look for clues from the plants themselves to help you decide when to fertilize. The yellowing of older (bottom) leaves, for example, may mean a deficiency of nitrogen. This is often accompanied by other leaves turning light green. Burnt-looking leaf tips and dark green or reddish purple lower leaves may mean a phosphorus deficiency. Too little potassium may scorch or wilt old leaves.

Plants will also tell you if you've given them too much fertilizer. Necrosis, for example, is a result of too much fertilizer. It begins with browning of the tips of the leaves. Known as "fertilizer burn," the browning proceeds along the edges of the leaf to the leaf base. Because of the relatively small volume of growing medium, container plants are more likely to suffer from overfertilization than in-ground plants. If you believe you've overdone it, flush out the excess fertilizer by running water through the potting mix.

Synthetic Versus Organic

The aisles of most garden centers are filled with many brands of synthetic fertilizer. They are popular with container gardeners because they are easy to use and fast-acting. There are, however, some negatives. Synthetics are often made from natural gas and use lots of electricity during their manufacture, especially those where the nitrogen component is some form of ammonia, such as ammonium nitrate and ammonium phosphate. Another ingredient, phosphorous, often comes from phosphate rock, the mining and processing of which can cause pollution and environmental damage.

In addition, synthetic fertilizers are water soluble and leach from the soil quickly. In ground-based gardens and on lawns, the leaching of water-soluble fertilizers often leads to pollution of ponds and streams. In containers, this is less of a problem because the scale is smaller, but using water-soluble fertilizers still results in a lot of nutrients running out the drain holes of your pots.

Gardener's Tip

Organic fertilizers are more forgiving than synthetics. You're less likely to overfertilize or to burn your plants. They also break down completely and do not contribute to the buildup of growth-inhibiting salts in your containers. They do, however, require the presence of microbes to break down nutrients to a form plants can use.

Fish emulsion fertilizer (above) is my preferred way to provide supplementary nutrition to containers of all types. Mix the solution according to the manufacturer's directions, and apply to roots or to leaves (right). Apply supplemental doses of granular fertilizer by digging a trough at the container's perimeter, filling with fertilizer (below), and covering with potting mix.

Organic fertilizers, on the other hand, are made from organic materials. Bone meal, dried blood, manures, worm castings, and green sand are commonly used ingredients. I prefer to mix bone meal, dried blood, and green sand into my potting mix and to make supplemental feedings, as necessary, with a liquid fish- and seaweed-based fertilizer. The latter has a bit of an odor, but it dissipates quickly. For organic fruits and vegetables, organic fertilizers are, of course, the only way to go.

Drawback to Organics

Despite their environmental appeal, organic fertilizers have some drawbacks for container gardeners. The main one is that they require microbes to help break down the nutrients and make them available to your plants. While this is not a big deal when gardening in the ground, where it's rel-

atively easy to maintain microbes in the soil, it can be a challenge in containers, where there are often big swings in moisture and temperature. It's also a problem if your potting mix is lean on compost, as many potting mixes are. The organic material found in compost is what supports microbial life.

If you opt for using organic fertilizers, strive to maintain moist conditions and even temperatures. Using drip irrigation and large containers will help. Adding compost, manure, and garden soil to your potting mix will also help. Avoid using too much compost or soil because the mix may lose its "structure," the small subsurface pores

Plants that grow slowly such as the hinoki cypress bonsai (opposite) need much less fertilizer than plants that bloom for an entire season or that bear fruit.

Fertilizer Basics

Fertilizers, whether organic or synthetic (inorganic), are graded so that consumers can better judge what they're buying. The fertilizer grade is the prominent three numbers on the container. The numbers refer to the percentage of macronutrients, or primary nutrients: nitrogen (N), phosphorus (P), and potassium (K). They are almost always printed in the N-P-K order. So, if the fertilizer grade is 10-4-3, 10 percent of the product is nitrogen, 4 percent is phosphorous, and 3 percent is potassium. The remaining 83 percent is filler and is inert.

Nitrogen is the most important of all nutrients. It promotes the growth of leaves and stems and gives leaves a healthy dark green color. Phosphorous stimulates the formation and growth of roots and supports vigorous growth, flowering, and seed development. Potas-

sium helps plants resist disease and increases vigor and hardiness.

The ratio of nutrients is important in determining what fertilizer to use on your plants. Plants grown for foliage, for example, require a higher ratio of nitrogen; plants grown for flowers and fruits need extra phosphorous.

The actual amount of N, P, and K by weight helps determine application rates. A 16-ounce container of 10-4-3 fertilizer, for example, contains about 1.6 ounces of nitrogen. Refer to the manufacturer's recommendation when figuring out how much fertilizer to use and how often.

In addition to the primary nutrients, fertilizers contain micronutrients, or secondary nutrients. Secondary nutrients include calcium, magnesium, and sulfur, all of which are important to plant health. Calcium, for example, helps roots and shoots develop and aids in pollen development. The con-

tents label on fertilizer containers should list secondary nutrient percentages. If not, check the maker's Web site. Micronutrients that are necessary only in very small amounts include boron, copper, chlorine, iron, manganese, molybdenum, and zinc.

Fertilizers are available in granular and liquid forms. Granular fertilizers can be mixed with potting soil prior to planting. Liquid fertilizers can be applied to containers throughout the growing season by adding them to your watering can before watering. Fertilizers can be water soluble or insoluble. Soluble fertilizers dissolve in water and tend to leach out of containers quickly. Insoluble fertilizers take some time to break down, usually through microbial digestion. Soluble fertilizers are synthetic, or inorganic; insoluble fertilizers are organic.

that hold air and retain water. If this happens, the mix will compact, and the roots may suffocate and rot. One part compost and/or soil to four parts potting mix is a safe ratio. You may also buy organic potting mixes that have been inoculated with microbes. Other products allow you to add microbes directly to your potting mix, usually in the form of a dry powder or liquid "tea."

A second drawback to organic fertilizers is that concentrations of nutrients tend to be low. Fish and kelp emulsions, for example, typically have a 2-5-1 grade. (See "Fertilizer Basics" on page 138.) This means that a 32-ounce bottle will yield less than an ounce of nitrogen. Furthermore, many organic fertilizers are incomplete. They may contain a high percentage of one nutrient but not much, if any, of another. Dried blood with a 12-0-0 grade, for example, contains a significant amount of nitrogen but no phosphorous or potassium. Bone meal with a 4-12-0 grade is loaded with phosphorus but contains no potassium. Green sand, sourced from ancient marine fossil deposits, is a common organic used for supplying potassium and iron. With grades as low as 0-0-1, you'd obviously need to use a lot of it to equal what you can get from a 10-10-10 bag of synthetic fertilizer.

Advances in Organic Fertilizer

Several organic fertilizer makers have introduced products that combine vegetable and animal protein meals and naturally occurring minerals for a more complete and convenient-to-use product. I use a 5-5-5 all-purpose organic fertilizer and get good results. For supplemental liquid applications, I prefer a 2-4-1 hydrolysate (liquid compound) that's made from fresh fish for my edibles. It has little or no odor and is more nutritionally balanced than fish emulsion fertilizers. For my ornamental containers, I use light, regular applications of a water-soluble synthetic fertilizer. Next year, however, I plan to try a recently introduced, nitrogen-rich concentrate that is made from beets. Note: just because an organic fertilizer is in liquid form doesn't mean that nutrients will be immediately available to your plants. As with any organic fertilizer, microbes are necessary to convert the nutrients to a form plants can use.

Heavy feeders, including corn (left) and eggplant (opposite), may require weekly feedings with a water-soluble fertilizer.

*Large amounts of fossil fuels
are expended in the production
of synthetic fertilizers. Use organic
products when possible.*

Pinching and Pruning

Plants in containers need occasional grooming to look their best. Many annuals and perennials, for example, will continue to bloom longer if you remove withered blossoms, a chore referred to as "deadheading." Simply pinch off blossoms with your fingers. If it's too tough to pinch the flower stems, snip them with a pair of shears or clippers. Cut as close to the flower-stem base as possible.

For plants with many small blossoms, which makes it too tedious to pinch each flower individually, you may want to wait until most of the flowering is done and then shear off the remaining flowers, dead or alive. Many shorn plants will begin to set new buds after a couple of weeks. While you're at it, snip off any dead or diseased leaves and stems. This will not only improve the plant's appearance but make it less vulnerable to disease.

Some fall flowers, such as mums, may grow too tall for their containers. They look awkward, and they're likely to topple over in a stiff wind. In addition to providing some support in the way of a cage or stake, cutting back the plants a couple of times during the summer will ensure multiple blossoms and more compact growth.

Cutting back will also increase production of edible plants, such as herbs. Once your plants are established, pinch the main stem. The plant will eventually fill out with new branches. If flowers appear, pinch them off, too. When the plants are large and full, you can cut off large quantities of herbs for immediate use, or dry or freeze some for the winter. Cutting back, as long as it's still early in the season, will encourage new growth.

Some flowering plants will perform an encore, if you're patient. Look for new growth at the base of a spent plant. Trim away the old growth to make room for the new. You can also plant the new growth in your garden to free the pot for a new planting.

Pruning promotes plant health and improves shape. Cut away dead, damaged, and diseased growth. Remove excess branches that run through the plant's center, too. Doing so will improve air circulation, allow sunlight to infiltrate, and help eliminate branches that rub in the wind—a cause of infection and rot.

When shaping a shrub or tree by pruning, cut back branches at varying lengths for a more natural look. Make the cuts at branch unions or just above buds. Buds usually grow in the direction they point, so if you

Pruning Basics

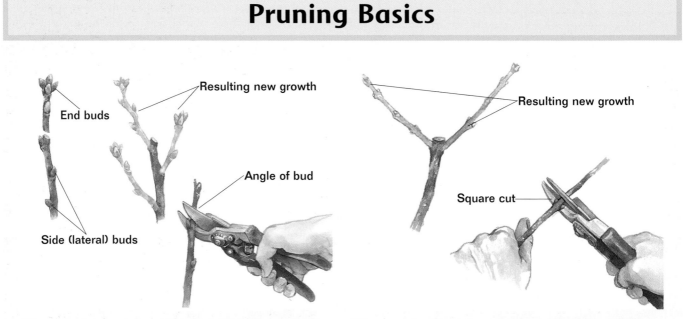

When pruning branches with alternate buds, choose a bud pointing in the direction you want a branch, and make a cut about ¼ in. above and parallel with the bud.

When pruning branches with opposite buds, cut perpendicular to the branch, just clear of the bud tip. This will result in fairly even growth of both buds.

cut above a bud that is pointing outward from the plant, that will likely be the direction of the new growth. (See "Pruning Basics," opposite.) Make your cut at the same angle as the bud.

Thinning a shrub or tree helps promote flowering but does not significantly change its shape. It typically involves the removal of entire branches. When cutting off a branch from a main stem, do not leave a stub. This is an open invitation to disease. Do not cut too close to the main stem either. Branches have a collar at their base from which healing will take place, as long as it's left intact.

It is important to research the plant before you begin cutting. Spring-flowering shrubs, such as lilacs and andromeda, bloom on one-year-old growth. You may prune to thin them in early spring, but don't overdo it, or you'll have few blooms in the spring. After the shrubs bloom, remove the flowers to conserve the plant's energy that would otherwise be spent on seedpod and seed development. Summer-flowering shrubs, including wisteria and hydrangeas, bloom on same-year growth. Prune them in late winter or early spring before the growth begins. Some shrubs grow so quickly they can survive poor pruning. Others, such as azaleas, grow so slowly that they may not regain shape after a careless cut for years. For vigorous growers, such as vines, you may prune anytime. Don't be timid. Vines such as wisteria and honeysuckle are practically unstoppable. Once again, cutting the main and secondary stems will generate more lateral growth and often second and third sets of buds and blooms.

Root Pruning

Potted trees and shrubs that have reached the size you desire can often be maintained at that size, in the same pot, by root pruning. Simply pull the plant from its container and examine the roots. If they have filled the pot, cut away about 1 or 2 inches of the root mass on all sides and at the bottom. Renew the potting mix, add fertilizer, and replant. This way, the plant will have space for roots to find new sources of nutrients, and the mix will be better able to retain moisture.

If you want a potted tree or shrub to grow larger, there's less need to prune its roots. If the roots are tightly bound, score them with a knife to a depth of about ½ inch and loosen the root-ball. Then repot in a new, larger container. Apply mulch to plants you've root-pruned, and water them daily for the first week. Root pruning is best done in spring.

Gardener's Tip

Late winter or early spring is generally the best time to prune deciduous plants. You can see the branch structure, and cuts will have time to heal before winter. Prune fast-growing plants at any point in the season but not during the hottest part of the day.

Snip or pick off withered blossoms to get the most of annuals and many perennials. Called "deadheading," it will promote new blossoms and extend your container show.

Replacing Plants

As seasons change, some annuals will begin to look tired—or worse. Or you may simply grow tired of them. In either case, it's a relatively simple matter to replace spent plants. Carefully pry the plants up with a trowel, trying not to disturb the ones you plan to leave in place. If the roots are entwined with adjacent plants, use a serrated knife to separate them. Then slip in the new neighbor, tamp, and water.

A typical replacement for spring annuals in my garden would be to replace pansies with petunias, impatiens, or vinca. Of course, you may choose to pull out your entire display and start over for the summer or fall seasons.

You may also choose to move the container that's no longer blooming to a less prominent spot. If you've included plants with handsome foliage, it will still look attractive. It just won't be the current star.

Removing a spent plant is sometimes easier said than done. A serrated knife is often helpful. Here leggy violas are making way for dwarf zinnias.

Pests and Diseases

No matter what you do, plant pests and diseases are going to be a part of your gardening experience. Container gardening, however, allows you much more control over your plants' environment than does in-ground gardening. Sterile potting soils and clean pots reduce the chance of problems. Infestations are much easier to monitor in potted plants, too. Keep in mind, however, that insects and fungal spores are always present and can attack even in a controlled environment. Here are some easy precautions to limit your exposure to invasion.

1 Do not reuse potting mixes from containers that were host to insects or contaminated by disease-causing funguses or bacteria. To avoid reintroducing problems next year, remove the suspect potting soil, break it into pieces, and toss it in the compost bin.

2 Clean your containers at the start of the new season, for the same reason. A good scrubbing with a solution of liquid detergent and water should be enough. For pots that may be contaminated with fungus, immerse them in a solution of one part household bleach to 10 parts water for about an hour. Then rinse the container thoroughly.

3 When purchasing your plants, always look for healthy specimens, and give them a good shower with the hose before planting.

4 Keep plants healthy by knowing their preferences. Giving them the right amounts of sun, water, and fertilizer will help them fend off insects and diseases. Remove plant debris, and maintain good air circulation, too.

5 Isolate or destroy infected plants to limit their exposure to healthy plants. Be sure to wash your tools and hands after handling infected plants. This may mean leaving a space between plants and walls and fences as well as between containers.

6 Know the difference between the good guys and the bad guys. Some bugs are beneficial to your plants. Ladybugs, ground beetles, and lacewings are a few that will consume plant-eating pests. Bad guys, if caught early, are easier to manage.

Gardener's Tip

Planted containers may look lovely to you, but to deer most look like dinner. For containers more than a step or two away from the house, the best deterrent is a 6- to 8-foot-tall fence. Two 3- or 4-foot fences, 3 feet apart are also effective. Other deterrents include sprays that make plants taste or smell bad and motion-activated water sprayers.

Insects: the Good and the Bad

1 **Good: Newly hatched lacewings prey on aphids and other soft-bodied pests.**

2 **Bad: Aphids suck plant juices from their hosts, often transmitting viral diseases as they do.**

3 **Bad: Thrips, which are tiny, lay eggs in plant tissue. They can stunt or distort plant growth.**

4 **Bad: Look for whiteflies feeding on the undersides of leaves. This is also a favored hiding spot for aphids.**

5 **Bad: Adult and nymph mealybugs suck plant juices. A sprayed-on oil-and-soap solution will get rid of them.**

6 **Good: Ladybugs are beneficial insects that feed on aphids and other soft-bodied insect pests.**

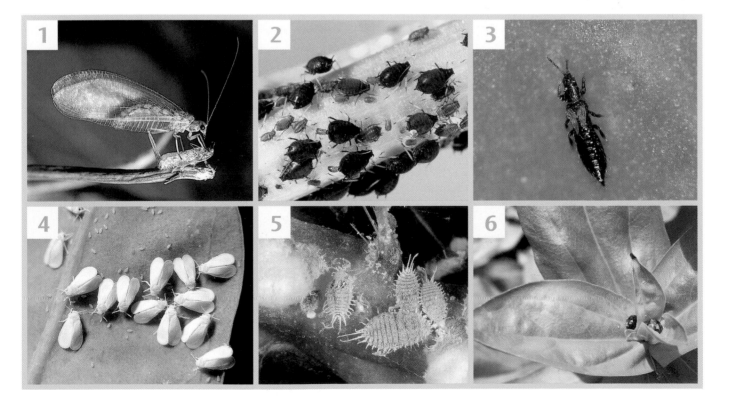

Common Insect Pests and Remedies

When watering, examine your plants for bugs and diseases. Remove any dead leaves or flowers, which make perfect homes for hatching eggs. Make sure your pots are lifted off the ground and are not sitting in stagnant water. A lot of the larger pests, including slugs, caterpillars, beetles, and weevils, can simply be picked off your plants and disposed of in a bucket of soapy water. Smaller insects, such as aphids and whiteflies, can be removed with a strong blast from your garden hose. Or you can dip a cotton swab in rubbing alcohol and apply it directly to the insects.

Larger or stubborn insect infestations can be treated with homemade remedies, which are less damaging than pesticides to your plants and the environment. Here's a recipe for a spray solution that will kill most soft-bodied insects, such as whiteflies, mealybugs, and aphids:

½ teaspoon dishwashing liquid
¼ teaspoon cooking oil
1 quart warm water

Oils work by coating insects and causing them to suffocate. It's unclear why soaps work. Perhaps it's because they compromise the insect's cells. Or it may be because they dissolve the wax coating on the insect's shell.

Add irritants, such as garlic or hot pepper, to make the potion a little more potent. For hard-shelled bugs, such as beetles and thrips, add two teaspoons of citrus oil or peppermint extract to the mixture. Insects, as well as rodents, have a strong dislike for peppermint extract.

The drawback to this spray is that you must hit the insect with the solution in order for it to work, so bugs hiding in curled leaves or crevices will not be affected. For best results, spray every 10 days. Avoid spraying during periods of direct sun. Rinse the solution from plants two or three hours after spraying to avoid damage to foliage. For more delicate plants, test a small section to ensure plant hardiness before spraying the entire plant.

Common Diseases and Remedies

Plant diseases are caused by funguses, viruses, or bacteria. Fungal diseases are the most common, though they spread slowly. If you react quickly you can save your plants. Typical symptoms are wilting or spotted leaves and rot, which can affect any part of the plant. Fungus problems are more common during a rainy season because funguses like warm, wet leaves. Both mold and mildew are forms of fungus. To avoid fungal problems, remove dead leaves and debris from around your plants. Separate your containers for good air circulation. Moving plants so they get more

Gardener's Tip

When using sprays against insects, remember to aim at the "bad" insects and not at ladybugs or other beneficial insects. Avoid toxic chemical pesticides entirely.

Spray leaves with an oil-and-soap solution to kill soft-bodied bugs, such as aphids, mealybugs, and white flies. Be sure to spray under leaves, where insects hide.

You can battle insects and diseases with relatively innocuous substances, including dish soap, vegetable oil, vinegar, garlic, and baking soda.

Common Plant Diseases

1 Powdery mildew on zucchini can be stopped by spraying with a milk and water solution.

2 This tomato's case of blossom-end rot was caused by a calcium imbalance.

3 Bacterial soft rot kills tissues, which become slimy and give off a foul odor.

4 Excess nitrogen stimulates bacterial blight, often in legumes.

5 Botrytis blight is also known as gray mold because fuzzy gray spores emerge.

6 Bacterial spot appears on green fruits. Small, dark spots form on leaves.

hours of sunshine will also help combat fungal diseases. Sprays made from water mixed with milk, baking soda, garlic, or apple cider vinegar are also effective.

When cases are severe, spray with a fungicide. You can make your own by following the soap/oil recipe on page 146 and then adding two tablespoons of baking soda.

Other fungicide recipes include mixing one teaspoon of mouthwash in one quart of warm water, or mixing one tablespoon of hydrogen peroxide in one gallon of water. These all should be mixed in the sprayer and applied every day until the fungus is gone. Your local garden supplier or home center will also carry an assortment of fungicides.

Viruses, which are usually spread by insects, are not as common as funguses, but once they take hold of your plant, they can destroy it quickly. If your plant leaves yellow, twist, and crinkle and suddenly the plant dies, the disease was most likely caused by a virus. In such cases, remove the infected plant.

Bacteria is the least common cause of plant disease. It does not easily infect plants. If your plants are healthy, they will ward off infections naturally because bacteria needs a mangled or broken leaf to invade the plant. If the plant is infected, bacteria causes soft rot in the plant tissues. The affected area may appear slimy. In case of infection, destroy the affected plants, and clean tools and pots thoroughly to prevent the bacteria from spreading.

Cut yellowed and mottled leaves from the bottom of vegetables, such as tomatoes, to slow the spread of disease. In most cases, this will enable an affected plant to survive through harvest.

Prepping for Winter

In cold climates, empty containers that were planted with annuals, including vegetables. Toss plants in the compost pile, and save the potting mix you can shake loose for next year. Be sure to save any bulbs you may have planted! They can be easy to miss when hidden in a mass of roots. Store the pots in a shed or garage, or leave them outdoors, upside down.

For perennials, trees, and shrubs, you have several options, depending upon their hardiness and the zone in which you live. One is to replant hardy plants in the garden. (In-ground soil temperatures don't get nearly as frigid as potting mix in an unprotected container.) I do this with perennials. It's also easier to insulate plants when they're in the ground using stakes, burlap, and mulch.

It's easiest, of course, to leave your hardy plants outside, in their containers (assuming they are freeze-proof). Insulate these containers with bubble wrap, plastic bags filled with crumpled newspaper or leaves, heaps of mulch or hay, or other similar insulating materials. Once your containers are insulated, push them together for additional protection. For wind protection, wrap the stems and branches with several layers of burlap. Plant protector bags, made of breathable fabrics, are also available.

Move less-hardy plants inside. I have overwintered hibiscus and mandevilla in the basement by a small window. All they require is water every couple of weeks. Unheated sheds, garages, and porches may be a plant storage option in climates that experience only light frost.

Keeping the Bugs Out

To avoid bringing insects into your home for the winter, it's wise to take a few precautions. First, spray insecticidal soap on the plant foliage several weeks before you plan to bring your plants indoors. Spray them again two weeks later. As the "move date" approaches, examine the plants and containers for bugs, and wash foliage with the hose. If you see any insects, try running several gallons of hot water (110–120° F) through the potting mix. When the plants are fully drained and dry, bring them indoors. Save your back by using a two-person sling, a dolly, or a hand truck to move large pots—and remember to lift with your legs (bent knees), not your back! You may want to keep your outdoor plants quarantined from indoor plants until you're sure they are free and clear of bugs.

While many plants' roots are unharmed by frozen ground, which stays at about 27° F, container-bound plants may suffer far colder temperatures. Insulate inside of containers with extruded polystyrene insulation. It cuts easily by scoring and snapping with a utility knife.

Insulate round containers with several layers of sill plate gasket (shown) or bubble wrap. Create an access hole in the wrapping for air circulation and for watering. Cover insulation with burlap.

Winter Checklist

When winter approaches, container gardeners must prepare. Here is a list of reminders that will have you ready to begin afresh when spring finally returns.

- Remove plant debris and mulch from pots because it may harbor insect eggs and disease spores.
- Cut back plants that require it, such as flowering vines and roses.
- Limit the sun and wind exposure of plants that will overwinter outdoors. Place them in a protected corner, near a wall if possible. Wrap stems and branches with burlap or garden fleece. Spray evergreen foliage with an anti-transpirant to protect against desiccation.
- Insulate containers to protect roots if you live in zones where temperatures can fall below 20° F for extended periods.
- Remove bulbs and tubers from containers. Label and store tender bulbs in ventilated containers for use next year. Egg cartons do the job nicely.
- Empty and store containers that are not made of frost-proof materials, including terra-cotta.
- Drain drip-irrigation systems if you live in an area subject to freezing.

Gardener's Tip

To protect roots from freezing weather (as well as from overheating), insulate the outside or the inside of containers prior to planting. For square containers, use rigid polystyrene insulation. For large round containers, use bubble wrap or sill-plate gasket.

Appendix

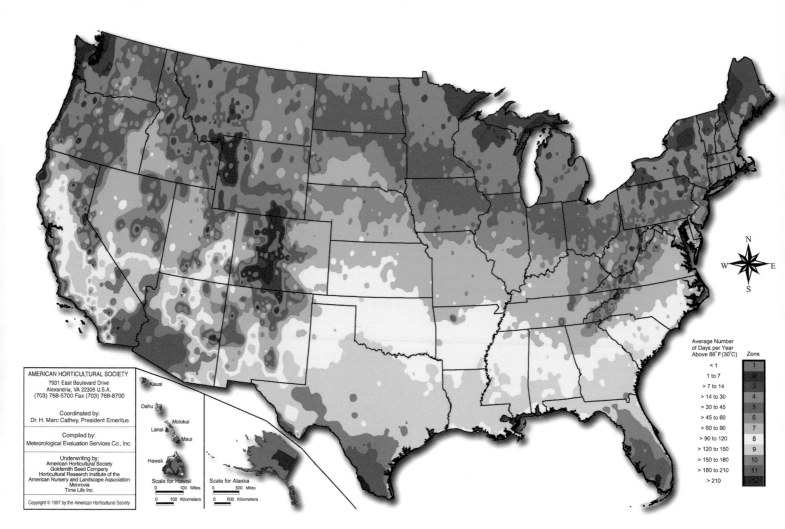

THE AMERICAN HORTICULTURAL HEAT-ZONE MAP

The American Horticultural Society (AHS) Heat-Zone Map divides the United States into 12 zones based on the average annual number of days a region's temperatures climb above 86°F, the temperature at which the cellular proteins of plants begin to experience injury. Introduced in 1998, the map is especially helpful for gardeners in southern and transitional zones. Nurseries, growers, and other plant sources list both cold hardiness and heat-tolerance zones for plants, including grasses. Using the United States Department of Agriculture (USDA) Plant-Hardiness Map, which can help determine a plant's cold tolerance, and the AHS Heat-Zone Map, gardeners can safely choose grasses that tolerate their region's lowest and highest temperatures.

Average Annual Minimum Temperature		
Temp. (°C)	Zone	Temp. (°F)
−45.6 & below	1	below −50
−42.8 to −45.5	2a	−45 to −50
−40.0 to −42.7	2b	−40 to −45
−37.3 to −40.0	3a	−35 to −40
−34.5 to −37.2	3b	−30 to −35
−31.7 to −34.4	4a	−25 to −30
−28.9 to −31.6	4b	−20 to −25
−26.2 to −28.8	5a	−15 to −20
−23.4 to −26.1	5b	−10 to −15
−20.6 to −23.3	6a	−5 to −10
−17.8 to −20.5	6b	0 to −5
−15.0 to −17.7	7a	5 to 0
−12.3 to −15.0	7b	10 to 5
−9.5 to −12.2	8a	15 to 10
−6.7 to −9.4	8b	20 to 15
−3.9 to −6.6	9a	25 to 20
−1.2 to −3.6	9b	30 to 25
1.6 to −1.1	10a	35 to 30
4.4 to 1.7	10b	40 to 35
4.5 & above	11	40 & above

THE USDA PLANT HARDINESS MAP

The United States Department of Agriculture (USDA) Plant-Hardiness Map divides the United States into 11 zones according to average minimum winter temperatures. Hardiness zones are used to identify regions to which grasses are suited based on their cold tolerance. Many factors, such as elevation and moisture level, come into play when determining whether a grass is suitable for your region. Local climates may vary from what is shown on the map. Contact your local Cooperative Extension Service for seed recommendations for your area.

Plant Hardiness Zones	
0a	4a
0b	4b
1a	5a
1b	5b
2a	6a
2b	6b
3a	7a
3b	7b
	8a

Canada's Plant Hardiness Map outlines the different zones in Canada where various types of grasses will most likely survive. It is based on the average climatic conditions of each area. The hardiness map is divided into nine major zones: the harshest is 0 and the mildest is 8. Relatively few plants are suited to zone 0. Subzones (e.g., 4a or 4b, 5a or 5b) are also noted in the map legend. These subzones are most familiar to Canadian gardeners. Some significant local factors, such as micro-topography, amount of shelter, and subtle local variations in snow cover, are too small to be captured on the map. Year-to-year variations in weather and gardening techniques can also have an impact on plant survival in any particular location.

Resource Guide

All Decked Out
200 W. 16th St., Apt. 7J
New York, NY 10011
212-807-7458
www.alldeckedoutnyc.com
A gardening installation and maintenance company that special-izes in urban gardens and landscapes.

Aquascape, Inc.
901 Aqualand Wy.
St. Charles, IL 60174
866-877-6637
www.aquascapeinc.com / www.rainxchange.com
Manufactures the RainXchange rainwater harvest system, a barrel that captures and reuses our most precious resource.

Campo de' Fiori
1815 N. Main St., Rt. 7
Sheffield, MA 01257
413-528-1857
www.campodefiori.com
Designs and creates handmade pots and planters using natural materials, with an emphasis on terra-cotta and stone.

Chicago Specialty Gardens
688 Milwaukee Ave., Ste. 304
Chicago, IL 60642
312-243-7140
www.chicagogardens.com
A full-service firm that specializes in creating landscape and rooftop gardens.

EarthBox
1350 Von Storch Ave.
Scranton, PA 18509
888-917-3908
www.earthbox.com
A self-watering planter that works well for larger plants, such as tomatoes.

EcoForms
4520 Thomas Rd.
Sebastopol, CA 95472
707-823-1577
www.ecoforms.com
Durable, sustainable containers (made from renewable grain husks) that are an alternative to plastic pots.

Ferry-Morse Seed Company
601 Stephen Beale Dr.
Fulton, KY 42041
800-626-3392
www.ferry-morse.com
Seventh-generation company that offers seeds, seed-starting kits, and potting mixes. Their Web site has gardening tips.

Four Seasons Container Gardens
13009 N.W. Corso Ln.
Portland, OR 97229
503-629-8410
www.fourseasonscontainergardens.com
Designs, installs, and maintains container gardens. Their design consultants help you find the right pots and the right plants.

Gardener's Supply Company
128 Intervale Rd.
Burlington, VT 05401
888-833-1412
www.gardeners.com
Designs and sells a wide range of garden supplies, including self-watering planters, hanging planters, and window boxes.

Learn2Grow
1655 Palm Beach Lakes Blvd., Ste. 800
West Palm Beach, FL 33401
561-209-6544
www.learn2grow.com
Online database of over 10,000 plants that includes photos and recommended growing conditions.

The following list of manufacturers and associations is meant to be a general guide to additional industry and product-related sources. It is not intended as a listing of products and manufacturers represented by the photographs in this book.

Netherlands Flower Bulb Information Center/North America
Ethan Allen Hwy.
Danby, VT
802-293-2852
www.bulb.com
Provides information about selecting and growing many types of bulbs.

Ocean Crest Seafoods, Inc.
P.O. Box 1183
Gloucester, MA 01931
800-259-4769
www.neptunesharvest.com
Manufactures Neptune's Harvest Fish Fertilizer, which is made from North Atlantic fish.

Ore Designs Inc.
130 S. Redwood Rd., Ste. G
North Salt Lake, UT 84054
801-936-0499
www.orecontainers.com
Designs and manufactures a line of containers that have a minimal impact on the environment. Catalog available online only.

Packing Pearls
13009 N.W. Corso Ln.
Portland, OR 97229
503-629-8410
www.packingpearls.com
Reusable, lightweight pot fillers designed to keep soil in while allowing air and water to flow through the pot.

Plant Health Care, Inc.
440 William Pitt Way
Pittsburgh, PA 15238
800-421-9051
www.planthealthcare.com
Manufactures Terra-Sorb, a potassium hydrogel that mixes into the soil to reduce watering frequency and drought stress.

Plow & Hearth
7021 Wolftown Hood Rd.
Madison, VA 22727
800-494-7544
www.plowhearth.com
National catalog, retail, and Internet company that offers gardening products, including a range of containers and planters.

The Pot de Deck
Bridgewater, NJ
908-635-2147
www.thepotdedeck.com
Designs, installs, and maintains container gardens on decks and enclosed patios.

Proven Winners
111 E. Elm St., Ste. D
Sycamore, IL 60178
877-865-5818
www.provenwinners.com
A leading brand of high-quality flowering plants. The company's Web site has container gardening information.

The Scott's Miracle-Gro Company
14111 Scottslawn Rd.
Marysville, OH 43041
888-270-3714
www.scotts.com
Provides lawn and garden products, including fertilizer, weed and insect control, plant food, and spreaders.

W. Atlee Burpee & Co.
300 Park Ave.
Warminster, PA 18974
800-333-5808
www.burpee.com
Offers plant, seeds, and soil test kits for determining nutrient and pH levels before you fertilize and plant.

Glossary

Acidic. Soil pH that is less than 7.0 (neutral); acid soils tend to be deficient in phosphorus and sometimes contain excess manganese and aluminum.

Alkaline. Soil pH that is above 7.0 (neutral); alkaline soils tend to lack manganese and boron.

Annual. A plant that germinates, grows, flowers, produces seeds, and dies in the course of a single growing season; a plant that is treated like an annual and grown for a single season's display.

Beneficial insects. Insects that are considered "helpful" in the garden because they kill pest insects. Examples include ladybugs and tachinid flies.

Biennial. A plant that flowers, produces seeds, and dies in its second growing season.

Bulbs. Globular masses of plant tissue (including undeveloped leaves, stem, and bud) that store food for some types of plants while they are dormant. Corms, rhizomes, and tubers are other types of storage organs that are often referred to as bulbs even though they are not. Spring planting bulbs, such as begonias, dahlias, and callas, are planted in the spring and bloom in the summer. Usually, they are not hardy in cold-weather climates. Fall bulbs, such as daffodils, tulips, and hyacinths, are planted in the fall before the first frost and bloom in the spring. They typically require a cold period to bloom.

Companion planting. Positioning plants in the garden to take advantage of their influence on neighboring plants. Can be used to stimulate growth or to ward off pests or disease.

Compost. A humus-rich, organic material formed by the decomposition of leaves, grass clippings, and other organic materials. Used to improve soil.

Compost tea. Liquid made by steeping compost in water; used as a fertilizer or treatment for fungal diseases on plants.

Conifer. Usually an evergreen, woody plant that bears cone-like fruit and has needle-shaped leaves.

Container. A decorative or utilitarian vessel in which plants may be grown. Common types of containers include pots, window boxes, troughs, urns, bowls, and baskets.

Cultivar. A cultivated variety of a plant, often bred or selected for some special trait, such as double flowers, compact growth, cold hardiness, or disease resistance.

Days to maturity. The number of days until a crop can be harvested. Days to maturity are often printed on seed packets and in catalogs, but these can cause confusion. Sometimes the numbers are from sowing. Sometimes they are from germination. Other times they are from the time seedlings are transplanted to the outdoors. In general, days from sowing or germination are used for vegetables that are planted outdoors directly from seed, such as beans, corn, and squash. Days from transplanting are used for plants that are usually started indoors or in the nursery, such as tomatoes, peppers, and eggplants.

Deadhead. To remove old flowers during the growing season to prevent seed formation and to encourage the development of new flowers.

Deciduous. A tree, shrub, or vine that drops all of its leaves in the fall or winter.

Double flower. A flower with more than the standard number of rows of petals.

Drip irrigation. A low-pressure system for irrigating container plantings, as well as gardens, shrubs, and lawns. Water is released slowly over longer periods of time by emitters or sprayers, and it is applied as close to plant roots as possible.

Evergreen. Either a broad-leaved plant or a conifer that retains foliage for at least one year.

Fertilizer. Inorganic material, such as gases and minerals, or organic materials, such as fish emulsion and manure, used primarily to provide nutrients for plants. All commercial fertilizers are required by law to state the minimum amount of nutrients supplied. An example is 5-1-2 (5 percent nitrogen, 1 percent phosphorus, and 2 percent potassium).

Fish emulsion. A natural, liquid fertilizer made from fish. The primary nutrient is nitrogen, but this fertilizer also supplies phosphorus and potassium.

Focal point. A landscape element, usually a plant or plant grouping that draws the attention of viewers.

Genus A closely related group of species sharing similar characteristics and probably evolved from the same ancestors. In scientific, or botanical, language the genus begins with an uppercase letter and is followed by the species name, which begins with a lowercase letter. Both words are italicized, as in *Acer palmatum*. The plural form of *genus* is *genera*.

Habit. The characteristic shape or form a plant assumes as it grows.

Harden off. To gradually acclimate indoor seedlings to outside conditions before transplanting.

Hardiness. A plant's ability to survive the winter without protection from the cold.

Hardiness zone. Geographic region where the coldest temperature in an average winter falls within a certain range, such as between 0° and –5°F.

Heat zone. A region determined by the average annual number of days its temperatures climb above 86°F.

Herbaceous. Perennial plants that die back to the ground each fall, then grow back again each spring.

Horticultural oil. Hydrocarbon-based pesticide derived from petroleum, plant fat, or animal fat. When sprayed on plants, it kills insects by smothering them or disrupting their metabolism. Use only in cool, shady conditions with low to moderate relative humidity.

Hybrid. A plant resulting from crossbreeding plants that belong to different varieties, species, or genera. Hybrids are indicated in scientific names by a multiplication sign (x) between the genus and species names.

Invasive plant. A plant that spreads quickly, often by runners, and mixes with or dominates adjacent plantings.

Loam. Natural or amended soil that is well structured, fertile, moisture retentive, and free draining. Loam contains a balanced mix of sand, silt, and clay particles, as well as organic matter.

Mulch. A layer of bark, peat moss, compost, shredded leaves, hay or straw, lawn clippings, gravel, paper, plastic, or other materials spread over the soil around the base of plants. During the growing season, mulch can help retard evaporation of moisture, inhibit weed growth, and moderate soil temperature variations. In the winter, a mulch of evergreen boughs, coarse hay, or leaves is used to protect plants from freezing.

Nutrients. Nitrogen, phosphorus, potassium, calcium, magnesium, sulfur, iron, and other elements needed by growing plants.

Peat moss. Partially decomposed mosses and sedges harvested from boggy areas and used in potting mixes.

Perennial. A plant that lives for a number of years, generally flowering each year. Plants that live for several years only in warm winter zones are called tender perennials and are treated as though they were annuals.

pH. Measure of acid/alkaline balance in soil that affects the availability of plant nutrients, such as phosphorus and potassium. Seven is neutral on the pH scale.

Potting mix. Typically a soilless mixture of peat moss, ground bark, perlite, or similar materials in which plants may be grown in containers. Mixes are formulated to maintain a mix of air and moisture and to promote good drainage. Sometimes, potting mixes include small amounts of fertilizer.

Rhizome. A horizontal underground stem, often swollen into a storage organ. Both roots and shoots emerge from rhizomes, which can be divided to make new plants.

Root ball. The mass of soil and roots dug up with a plant when it is removed from the ground or from a container.

Self-watering container. A pot or planter that includes a reservoir for water in its base and from which plants are irrigated. Moisture moves from the reservoir to the potting mix via capillary action or evaporation.

Single flower. A flower with a single concentric row of petals.

Species. A group of very similar plants that share many characteristics and can interbreed freely. In scientific, or botanical, language the species name always follows the genus name and begins with a lowercase letter, and both words are italicized.

Standard. A plant trained to grow a round, bushy head of branches atop a single upright trunk.

Index

Index

Photo Credits

Front cover: *right* Joe Provey/Home & Garden Editorial Services *left from top to bottom* Netherlands Flower Bulb Information Center, Joe Provey/Home & Garden Editorial Services, Roger A. Miller/Homescaper LLC/Four Seasons Container Gardens, Gardener's Supply, Georgianna Lane/Garden Photo World **page 1:** Proven Winners **page 2:** Ruth Zelig, design: Ruth Zelig/Pot de Deck **page 6:** *left* iStockphoto/Liza McCorkle *middle left* Ruth Zelig, design: Ruth Zelig/Pot de Deck *middle right* iStockphoto/Merlin Farwell *right* iStockphoto/Liza McCorkle **page 7:** Proven Winners **pages 8–9:** Joe Provey/Home & Garden Editorial Services **page 10:** iStockphoto/Liza McCorkle **page 12:** *top* iStockphoto/Captured-Nuance *bottom* Ruth Zelig, design: Ruth Zelig/Pot de Deck **page 14:** *bottom left* iStockphoto/Patty Steib *top right* Ruth Zelig, design: Ruth Zelig/Pot de Deck **page 15:** Joe Provey/Home & Garden Editorial Services **page 16:** *bottom left* iStockphoto/Merlin Farwell *bottom right* iStockphoto/David Scheuber **page 17:** Joe Provey/Home & Garden Editorial Services **page 18:** iStockphoto/Nancy Nehring **page 19:** Joe Provey/Home & Garden Editorial Services **page 20:** *top right* All Decked Out *bottom* Joe Provey/Home & Garden Editorial Services **page 21:** Chicago Specialty Gardens **page 22:** *left* Joe Provey/Home & Garden Editorial Services *top right* iStockphoto/Melissa Anne Galleries *bottom right* Ruth Zelig, design: Ruth Zelig/Pot de Deck **page 23:** Joe Provey/Home & Garden Editorial Services **page 24:** Ruth Zelig, design: Ruth Zelig/Pot de Deck **page 26:** iStockphoto/Laila Roberg **page 27:** Ruth Zelig, design: Ruth Zelig/Pot de Deck **pages 28–30:** Campo de' Fiori **page 31:** *top left and middle* Gardener's Supply *bottom left* Joe Provey/Home & Garden Editorial Services *top right* Gardener's Supply *bottom right* Ore Containers **page 32:** EarthBox **page 33:** iStockphoto/Stacey McRae **page 34:** Joe Provey/Home & Garden Editorial Services **page 35:** iStockphoto/River North Photography **page 36:** *left* Joe Provey/Home & Garden Editorial Services *right* Smith & Hawkins **page 37:** Joe Provey/Home & Garden Editorial Services **page 38:** Joe Provey/Home & Garden Editorial Services **page 39:** *top* Ore Containers *bottom* Joe Provey/Home & Garden Editorial Services **pages 40–41:** Joe Provey/Home & Garden Editorial Services **page 42:** Carl Weese/ Home & Garden Editorial Services **page 44:** Carl Weese/Home & Garden Editorial Services **page 45:** Canadian Sphagnum Peat Moss Association **page 46:** Joe Provey/Home & Garden Editorial Services **page 47:** Carl Weese/Home & Garden Editorial Services **page 48:** *top* iStockphoto/JungaR *bottom* Netherlands Flower Bulb Information Center **page 50:** Carl Weese/Home & Garden Editorial Services **page 51:** Campo de' Fiori **pages 52–53:** Carl Weese/Home & Garden Editorial Services **page 55:** Carl Weese/

Home & Garden Editorial Services **page 56:** Joe Provey/Home & Garden Editorial Services **pages 58–59:** Joe Provey/Home & Garden Editorial Services **page 61:** Joe Provey/Home & Garden Editorial Services **page 62:** Proven Winners **page 63:** iStockphoto/Schnuddel **page 64:** Joe Provey/Home & Garden Editorial Services **page 65:** Ruth Zelig, design: Ruth Zelig/Pot de Deck **page 66:** Netherlands Flower Bulb Information Center **page 67:** *top* Netherlands Flower Bulb Information Center *bottom* Joe Provey/Home & Garden Editorial Services **page 68:** Netherlands Flower Bulb Information Center **page 69:** *top* Netherlands Flower Bulb Information Center *bottom* Joe Provey/Home & Garden Editorial Services, design: Kate Parisi **pages 70–73:** Joe Provey/Home & Garden Editorial Services **page 74:** Proven Winners **page 75:** Joe Provey/Home & Garden Editorial Services, design: Marilyn Thorkilsen **page 76:** Netherlands Flower Bulb Information Center **page 77:** *top* Netherlands Flower Bulb Information Center *bottom* Proven Winners **pages 78–79:** Joe Provey/Home & Garden Editorial Services **page 80:** *top* Georgianna Lane/Garden Photo World *bottom* Ruth Zelig, design: Ruth Zelig/Pot de Deck **page 81:** Georgianna Lane/Garden Photo World **page 82:** iStockphoto/Reagan Knotts **page 83:** *top* Joe Provey/Home & Garden Editorial Services *bottom* Roger A. Miller/Homescaper LLC, design: Joanna Guzzetta & Jennifer Williams/Four Seasons Container Gardens **page 84:** *top* Joe Provey/Home & Garden Editorial Services, design: Kate Parisi *bottom* Bob La Pointe **page 85:** Ruth Zelig, design: Ruth Zelig/Pot de Deck **pages 86–87:** Proven Winners **page 88:** *top* Joe Provey/Home & Garden Editorial Services, design: Kate Parisi *bottom* Joe Provey/Home & Garden Editorial Services **page 89:** *top* Joe Provey/Home & Garden Editorial Services *bottom* Proven Winners **page 90:** Proven Winners **page 91:** *top* Proven Winners *bottom* Joe Provey/Home & Garden Editorial Services, design: Jackie Heller **page 92:** *top* Proven Winners *bottom* Roger A. Miller/Homescaper LLC, design: Joanna Guzzetta & Jennifer Williams/Four Seasons Container Gardens **page 93:** *left* Roger A. Miller/ Homescaper LLC, design: Joanna Guzzetta & Jennifer Williams/Four Seasons Container Gardens *right* Joe Provey/Home & Garden Editorial Services, design: Jackie Heller **page 94:** Proven Winners **page 95:** Marilyn Thorkilsen, design: Marilyn Thorkilsen **page 96:** Joe Provey/Home & Garden Editorial Services **page 98:** Carl Weese/Home & Garden Editorial Services **pages 99–100:** Joe Provey/Home & Garden Editorial Services **page 101:** *top left* Carl Weese/Home & Garden Editorial Services *top middle* Smith & Hawkins *top right, bottom left, and bottom middle* Carl Weese/Home & Garden Editorial Services *bottom right* Joe Provey/Home & Garden Editorial Services **pages 102–104:** Joe Provey/Home & Garden

Editorial Services **page 105:** *top* Joe Provey/Home & Garden Editorial Services, design: Kate Parisi *bottom* Joe Provey/Home & Garden Editorial Services **page 106:** Georgianna Lane/Garden Photo World **page 107:** Joe Provey/Home & Garden Editorial Services **page 108:** *top* iStockphoto/David Scheuber *bottom* Joe Provey/Home & Garden Editorial Services **page 109:** *top* iStockphoto/Merlin Farwell *bottom* Julie Sedwick **page 110:** Joe Provey/Home & Garden Editorial Services, design: Kate Parisi **pages 111–112:** Joe Provey/Home & Garden Editorial Services **page 113:** *top* Joe Provey/Home & Garden Editorial Services *bottom* Ruth Zelig, design: Ruth Zelig/Pot de Deck **page 114:** Roger A. Miller/Homescaper LLC, design: Joanna Guzzetta & Jennifer Williams/Four Seasons Container Gardens **page 117:** *left* iStockphoto/marg99ar *right* Proven Winners **page 119:** Joe Provey/Home & Garden Editorial Services **page 120:** Joe Provey/Home & Garden Editorial Services, design: Marilyn Thorkilsen **pages 121–122:** Joe Provey/Home & Garden Editorial Services **page 123:** *top* iStockphoto/ROMA-OSLO *bottom* John Glover **page 124:** *top* Gardener's Supply *bottom* Proven Winners **page 125:** *top* Roger A. Miller/ Homescaper LLC, design: Joanna Guzzetta & Jennifer Williams/Four Seasons Container Gardens *bottom* Georgianna Lane/Garden Photo World **page 126:** *top* Smith & Hawkins *bottom* Ruth Zelig, design: Ruth Zelig/Pot de Deck **page 127:** Bob La Pointe **page 128:** Joe Provey/Home & Garden Editorial Services **page 129:** Bob La Pointe **pages 130–132:** Joe Provey/Home & Garden Editorial Services **page 133:** *top* Joe Provey/Home & Garden Editorial Services *bottom* Gardener's Supply **page 135:** Joe Provey/Home & Garden Editorial Services **page 136:** Gardener's Supply **page 137:** Joe Provey/ Home & Garden Editorial Services **page 139:** Bob La Pointe **page 140:** EarthBox **page 141:** Joe Provey/Home & Garden Editorial Services **pages 143–144:** Joe Provey/Home & Garden Editorial Services **page 145:** *top left* Hans Pfletschinger/Peter Arnold *top middle and top right* Nigel Cattlin/Holt Studios/Photo Researchers *bottom left* J. H. Robinson/Photo Researchers *bottom middle* Michael Gadomski/Photo Researchers *bottom right* Joe Provey/Home & Garden Editorial Services **page 146:** Joe Provey/Home & Garden Editorial Services **page 147:** *top left, top middle, and bottom right* Joe Provey/Home & Garden Editorial Services *top right* Phil Degginger/Bruce Coleman *bottom left and bottom middle* Nigel Cattlin/Holt Studios/Photo Researchers **page 148–149:** Joe Provey/Home & Garden Editorial Services **page 158:** Joe Provey/Home & Garden Editorial Services, design: Maxine Greenberg **back cover:** *left* Georgianna Lane/Garden Photo World *top right* Chicago Specialty Gardens *bottom right* iStockphoto/Patty Steib

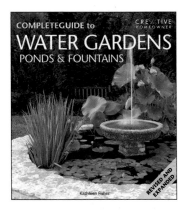

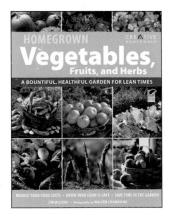
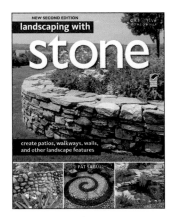